Actuarial Assessment of Child and Adolescent Personality:

An Interpretive Guide for the Personality Inventory for Children Profile

David Lachar, PhD and Charles L. Gdowski, PhD

Lafayette Clinic
and
Wayne State University

In collaboration with
Michael Butkus, M.S.
Sylvia Voelker, Ph.D.

PUBLISHED BY

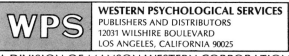

WESTERN PSYCHOLOGICAL SERVICES
PUBLISHERS AND DISTRIBUTORS
12031 WILSHIRE BOULEVARD
LOS ANGELES, CALIFORNIA 90025

A DIVISION OF MANSON WESTERN CORPORATION

Acturial Assessment of Child and Adolescent Personality:
An Interpretive Guide for the Personality Inventory for Children Profile

International Standard Book Number: 0-87424-305-X
Library of Congress Number: 79-129207

To Barbara and Alice
Their love of children has served as a constant inspiration.

LIST OF CONTENTS

LIST OF TABLES

LIST FIGURES

xi

FOREWORD

In his brief but pointed Foreword to the *Manual for the Personality Inventory for Children* (Wirt, Lachar, Klinedinst, & Seat, 1977), Starke R. Hathaway noted the inevitability of the comparison of the PIC to the MMPI, both being multidimensional inventories developed by staff and students at the University of Minnesota to appraise individuals in the midst of some emotional disturbance. The similarities are many and cogent (extensive range of content in the component items, true/false format, standard and special scales developed by means of a variety of scaling methods, a reference profile with high-ranging scores generally reflecting forms of psychopathology, based upon normally functioning comparison subjects, with a set of validity indicators to help determine the acceptability of any one protocol). The differences are just as important, however, and they may well be overlooked in any effort to evaluate the PIC and its growing body of validational research. It is necessary to keep in mind that the descriptions provided by the item endorsements in the PIC are, after all, not descriptions of the self by the respondent but descriptions of a child of whom some special knowledge is being conveyed to the clinician via these true or false answers. The PIC works to the extent that parents, relatives, or custodial adults show workable consistencies in the degree to which they know about, perceive, react to, judge, summarize, and are willing to report salient aspects of a youngster's manners, mood, comportment, successes, failures, habits, experiences, and involvements via these carefully worded statements. The years of careful empirical research by Robert D. Wirt and his colleagues and students at Minnesota attest to these useful consistencies. New concerns inevitably enter in trying to characterize a given child by means of PIC pattern, however, when degree of knowledge varies (mother versus father or grandmother), when level of socioeconomic status shifts the reference framework of "acceptable" behavior (fighting by young boys being seen as a necessity by low-status ghetto dwellers versus an embarrassing breach of decorum by middle-class suburban parents), or when pervasive values of an ethnic or cultural minority community affect the way children are viewed and judged (macho commitments in Latino barrios versus the scholarly veneration of literary or artistic heritages in Jewish communities). Test-taking attitudes take on new dimensions when a mother believes that full revelation of the faults of her boy will on the one hand assure proper attention for his difficulties from a supportive therapist or, on the other hand, will increase the likelihood of his being taken from her for placement in a foster home. These and other vital issues will play a role in the eventual development of the PIC into a valuable and trustworthy addition to the child clinician's armamentarium. This ontogeny of the PIC will necessarily continue to bear striking resemblance to the growth of the MMPI over the first four decades of its use even though it will inevitably encounter somewhat different developmental crises than those met by its older sister inventory. It is equally clear that the pace of its development in the age of computer-assisted administration, scoring, collating, and interpretation will be geometrically accelerated; witness the publication of the present validational compendium by Lachar and Gdowski a scant two years after the formal publication of the PIC test and manual. Work of comparable care and comprehensiveness on the MMPI accumulated only slowly; nothing of this sort emerged in the first two decades of MMPI research.

In the following chapters concurrent correlates of each component scale in the PIC from data about the child or adolescent's behavior in the family setting, school context, and psychiatric installation are summarized in unprecedented detail and precision. Rather than depending upon rule-of-thumb cutting scores as to the range of elevations in which clinical relevance is maximized (such as the primed versus unprimed scores in the MMPI profile), the present authors have empirically plotted the shifting frequencies of reported attributes over successive score elevations and thus can offer recommendations for the cutting scores to be employed when interpreting PIC profiles on comparable youngsters in other similar settings. No other assessment project has had available to it the resources in systematic reportage and computer-based retrieval that enable the psychometrician to assess simultaneously actual base-rates and significant increases over base-rate of attributes from three different perspectives on children and adolescents. In other clinical settings in which boys and girls with complicated behavioral and adaptational problems are routinely evaluated and helped, the data in the present compendium will be invaluable for the simple reason that the findings have been generated out of an on-going clinical service in which a multitude of practical concerns are uppermost and their resolution pressing to psychologist, psychiatrist, family therapist, social worker, probation officer, teacher, and parent alike.

A number of further questions will remain for users of the PIC (e.g., can the same instrument help assess change as well as appraise initial status, or will the parents' involvement in the treatment process that is so much more typical of child therapy inevitably spoil them as reporters of the new status of their child?; can the PIC generate a more coherent and workable taxonomy of child psychopathology out of the morass of competing systems of nosology now available in this fluid field, creating something akin to the MMPI classifications which many clinicians find more satisfactory than formal diagnostic categories now being regenerated in adult psychopathology?; how widely can the present set of scale correlates and cutting scores be generalized to new settings either more specialized than the Lafayette Clinic or drawing upon more select clients and patients from catchment areas more or less variable in urban sophistication, class differences, or ethnic diversity?). Additional questions could be raised about scale-by-scale approaches versus recurring configural patterns but most of these tactical issues have been already recognized by these knowledgeable and conscientious investigators themselves. There remains, however, the over-reaching issue in any effort to appraise a child's own contribution to the difficulties in which he or she is immersed: how much of the variance has its origins in the more or less stable attributes of the child and how does this component change over the course of personality development? Estimates of the variance in such quasi-stationary attributes vary from zero to over half of all the variance even for neonates and range upwards to totality over the ensuing years to adulthood. It should be clear that little effective progress towards answers to such questions in the various areas of child psychopathology will be achieved until research investigators and their clinical colleagues have in their possession objective assessment instruments which can help in this kind of partitioning of the data. With the PIC and its rapidly accumulating body of validational research becoming available, the picture is more optimistic than it has been for some years, at least since the appearance of comparable practical multidimensional instruments in the domain of intellective abilities (i.e., the WISC and WPPSI batteries).

The senior author of this volume carried out his dissertation project under the direction of Robert D. Wirt on an earlier version of the PIC and continued a close involvement with its development. Along with two other students of Professor Wirt (James K. Klinedinst and Philip D. Seat), David Lachar was a co-author of the PIC manual. At Minnesota, Lachar also became immersed in work with the MMPI and later carried out major research studies on it while in the Air Force at San Antonio, Texas. After moving to the Lafayette Clinic, Lachar gathered about him a group of enthusiastic and capable scientist-practitioners who were equally knowledgeable in clinical assessment and in computer-based data storage, analysis, and retrieval. A number of studies based on the MMPI and the PIC have already appeared from this research group. Lachar's co-author, Charles L. Gdowski, is also an outstanding example of this second generation of psychologists who combine clinical wisdom and experience with knowledge of modern data processing in meeting the current challenges of psychodiagnostic assessment. I look forward to many more contributions in this area from these authors and their colleagues at the Lafayette Clinic.

W. Grant Dahlstrom

Chapel Hill, North Carolina
April, 1979

PREFACE

This monograph is proof of our inability to conform to Dr. Starke R. Hathaway's recommendation that we should refrain from advocacy of the PIC and "permit the instrument to stand or fall on its own merits" (Wirt, Lachar, Klinedinst, & Seat, 1977, p.x.). In 1974 Roger Gudobba and James L. Grisell developed and installed at the Lafayette Clinic a computer assisted system that permitted informants to sort PIC items that were printed on computer cards, and provided automated processing of these responses. The ease by which PIC scores, critical items, and profiles could be obtained clearly influenced the decision to routinely administer this instrument in all Lafayette Clinic diagnostic evaluations of behaviorally disturbed children and adolescents. The fact that all PIC test data and independent correlate forms completed by parents, school personnel, and clinicians were routinely stored on computer tape, and were therefore accessible for further analysis, made this current project possible.

The ready availability of PIC scores and their association with rich and varied clinical data raised questions concerning test interpretation that could not be answered by what we had thought was a comprehensive, and even perhaps over-inclusive, test manual. Although the test manual documented the dimensions likely to be associated with each scale, it was not clear how high a scale elevation had to be before these characteristics could be accurately predicted. This and other questions were raised in the three years prior to the publication of the PIC. The answers, if we would take the history of the development of the MMPI as example, would be found in the conduct of multiple studies in many settings over several years, with the parallel development of a "clinical lore" for test interpretation. Even if we were to ignore the inherent problems with application of a PIC clinical lore, we were clearly too impatient to wait for its development. The study reported in this volume was designed to provide general interpretive guidelines for the PIC profile scales. We have been pleased by the results, and hope that other clinical investigators will initiate actuarial studies that will increase the utility of PIC indices.

These interpretive guidelines form the first stage results of a lengthy project that has required the support and efforts of many. First and foremost we wish to thank the mothers who served as test respondents and filled out questionnaires, the teachers, counselors and school social workers who provided observations and insights possible only within an educational context, and the many psychiatric residents who complied with changes in diagnostic procedures, and completed correlate forms, sometimes at no small inconvenience to themselves. The professional staff of the Division of Child and Adolescent Psychiatry at Lafayette Clinic, as well as administrative clinic personnel, gave generously of their time, and provided valuable insights that led to useful modifications of study design, form construction, and data interpretation. Research funds made available from the Michigan Department of Mental Health and Wayne State University facilitated data analysis. The contributions of Drs. Clyde B. Simson, Leonard R. Piggott, Lynda Hryhorczuk, Valerie Klinge, David Vander Vliet, James L. Grisell, Edward Meade, Allan DeHorn, Mark S. Goldman, R. Douglas Whitman, and Carolyn U. Shantz are greatly appreciated. Dr. Rochelle Robbins, Dr. Guy Doyal, Dr. William R. Nixon, and Manfred F. Greiffenstein volunteered their time to review this manuscript. The efficient collection and storing of data was made possible by the computer programming of Roger Gudobba, and the form development efforts of Elke Frankenberg. Charles A. Schauer, Frances Pipp, James R. Sharp, Willie Busby, and James P. Culbert spent numerous hours administering PICs. Mary Lash Pytiak helped distill voluminous computer printouts into manageable proportions, and aided in proofreading tables. Secretarial support was provided by Jacquline M. Anderson, Ophil Mann, Patricia L. Sahr, and Opal Barylski.

David Lachar
Charles L. Gdowski

Detroit, Michigan
August, 1978

CHAPTER 1

Introduction and Study Design

The publication of the Personality Inventory for Children (PIC) (Wirt, Lachar, Klinedinst, & Seat, 1977) offers a unique opportunity to construct actuarial interpretations of objective child personality scales. Profile scale characteristics presented in the PIC manual and recent studies of these scales (Gdowski, 1977; Lachar, Butkus, & Hryhorczuk, 1978; Lachar & Gdowski, 1979) suggest that such a project would prove effective in expanding the utility of the PIC.

The goal of this project has been to provide comprehensive information about individual profile scales, rather than correlates for total profiles classified through some nominal method, such as the MMPI code types (cf Lachar, 1974). Although some code type approach may eventually yield interpretations superior to those based on individual profile scale correlates (DeHorn, 1977; DeHorn, Lachar, & Gdowski, 1979), the current study sought to provide information applicable to all PIC profiles obtained in the evaluation of behaviorally disturbed children and adolescents. Actuarial interpretive systems based upon the profile code type have, unfortunately, proven of limited value because a significant proportion of profiles remain unclassified (cf Lachar, 1974, page 30).

Study Criteria

Criterion data were collected from *primary* informants, instead of from case files. It was hoped that systematic and direct inquiry of parents about developmental milestones, teachers about classroom behavior, and clinicians about judgments of neurological status and parental characteristics would reduce errors of omission and distortion which often plague the criterion collection process (cf. Gdowski, Lachar, & Butkus, 1980). These data were not collected by participants in a "research activity"; rather, form completion was introduced into the diagnostic process to enhance institutional goals. Criteria were collected from the sources that tradi-

1

tionally supply each class of facts, observations or judgments. Each form (see Appendix A) was constructed to take only a few minutes to complete, was designed for direct transmission to data processing format, and became a useful medical records document at the completion of each diagnostic evaluation. Although it would have been advantageous to collect identical information from two or more sources, in order to provide estimates of rating accuracy and behavior stability across settings, the judged importance of minimizing demands on each rater to maintain motivation, and hopefully, resultant accuracy, precluded this option. Each of the three basic sources of criteria are discussed below.

Preappointment Information. This form was completed by a child's guardian, usually a child's mother or both parents, to initiate a request for evaluation. It documented the behavior problems that motivated the parent to seek assistance, as well as behavior problem chronicity. In this study the dimension chronicity was not included; analyses were restricted to evaluation of the relationship between presence or absence of problem behaviors and scale elevation.

Information was also requested about developmental milestones achieved, as well as pregnancy, birth, and medical history. This procedure allowed parents the chance to reconsider their answers, and to check with other sources (e.g. in baby books, from grandparents and pediatricians, etc.) to verify the accuracy of their remembrances. Our evaluation of parents' recollections of developmental milestones led to placing more credence on observations of significant developmental delay, rather than early attainment. Each developmental item was, therefore, recorded as either within "normal limits," or as describing significant "delay." Delay was not established by reference to a general pediatric guide (cf Knobloch & Pasamanick, 1974); rather, distribution of study sample responses to the developmental items were examined, and decision rules were established that resulted in a conservative estimate of the prevalence of developmental delay in this sample. These thirteen developmental criteria classified an average of 13% of the study sample as significantly delayed for each milestone. Classification rates ranged from 4% (feed self) to 25% (ride a tricycle). The decision rules and classification rates for the developmental milestone data are presented below in Table 1-1.

Teacher Rating and School Information. Teachers and counselors readily completed this form to communicate their concerns and impressions. The final format was the product of consecutive refinement and consultation with school personnel. Teachers are excellent informants about child behavior as they are second in sheer amount of observation to only that of parents. In many instances, their observations of education-relevant behaviors (such as attention span and ability to handle abstract concepts) prove to be the most valuable in arriving at a diagnostic impres-

Table 1-1

Classification of Developmental Milestones

Developmental Item	Criteria of Significant Delay	Percent Classified
Birthweight	$\leq$ 88 ounces	10
Sit up	> 7 months	11
Crawl	> 9 months	9
Stand alone	>12 months	5
Walk by self	>15 months	11
Feed self	>24 months	4
Dress self	>49 months	8
Speak first real words	>18 months	24
Speak first real sentences	>34 months	20
Become completely toilet trained	>36 months	10
Help with household chores	>72 months	11
Ride a tricycle	>36 months	25
Tie own shoes	>66 months	23

sion and an effective disposition. In the present study, teachers were asked to complete a published behavior rating form (Walker, 1970), to rate age-appropriateness of academic achievement, to judge the reason(s) for problems observed, and indicate their recommendations for remediation. Appropriate additional material (e.g., psychological test reports) was also included when available.

Application Screening. Initial information from parents and school was evaluated to determine the appropriateness of each referral for psychiatric evaluation. This process resulted, in most cases, in the systematic restriction of study subjects to children with multiple behavioral problems. If review of the parent and school forms suggested parental overconcern, or a problem likely to be resolved by change of class placement, direct referral was frequently made to school psychologists or pediatric clinics. This study sample, therefore, included few children who presented either as normal, transiently maladjusted, or as cognitively deficient or academically retarded, without accompanying behavior problems.

Description of Current Problem Behaviors. This debriefing form was usually completed by a psychiatric resident following diagnostic interviews with child and parents, completion of a physical and neurological examination, and review of forms completed by both parents and teacher. Although the mode of form completion varied widely across raters, psychiatric residents were requested to complete the first three and one-half pages after completion of client interviews, but before the supervision of the evaluation with a staff psychiatrist. The final half page, which included diagnoses and recommendations, was to be completed following case supervision. This form recorded subjective judgments requiring specialized training (e.g., "separation anxiety," "inappropriate affect"), classified behavior problems in a fashion more detailed than was possible on the parent form (e.g., "speech disturbance" divided into articulation, phonation, rhythm, immature, stuttering or stammering, echolalia), guided the collection of medical data, and documented a substantial number of criteria reflecting interview behavior, parent characteristics, and present and past parental interaction.

Initial form elements were selected from several sources, most notably from the symptom list formulated by the Group for the Advancement of Psychiatry (1966). An attempt was made to establish and improve the reliability of this form by writing as many items as possible in behavioral terms, and by pretesting possible items in joint interviews conducted by the senior author and a fourth year child psychiatry resident. This pretesting led to: 1) the inclusion of a time limitation on most ratings to behaviors observed during the six months preceding the evaluation, 2) the addition of statements that clarified item intent (e.g., adding "in need of individual treatment" after the parent descriptor "emotionally disturbed," 3) removal of items when interrater agreement could not be met (e.g., substitution of "Expresses feelings of sadness or unhappiness" for "Depressed"), as well as 4) the evolution of an efficient item organization and checklist format. An admonition to avoid judgments not clearly supported by interview or history data was included in instructions to the rater. In this regard most checklist items included the option of omitting a rating when the data were insufficient.

Joint evaluation of 24 clients (12 children and 12 adolescents) by the senior author and a child psychiatry resident resulted in 87% agreement on the 134-item evaluative form. Examination of rater agreement on individual items, and the obtained frequency of checked behavior problems in this small sample, led to the removal of 26 items, the alteration of 36 other items, and the addition of 47 new rating elements. The latter included the addition of previous treatment for behavior problems, additional parental descriptors, and the recommendations/prognosis section of the final form.

The Description of Current Problem Behaviors form was organized around the following headings: self-concept, affect, cognitive functioning, interpersonal relations, physical development and health, family relations, parent description, diagnosis, and ideal recommendations. Pretesting of the final form revealed that it was not only relatively easy to complete, but that it also helped to organize observations, and thereby served as an instructive teaching aid. In addition, raters who tended to delay the dictation of their evaluations found that the completed form was of considerable assistance in formulating their clinical reports.

Subjects

The total sample of 431 children and adolescents was evaluated at Lafayette Clinic between December 1975 and April 1977. This sample of inpatients and outpatients consisted of 272 males, ranging in age from 2 to 17 years, and 159 females, ranging in age from 3 to 17 years. Two hundred subjects were under the age of thirteen (140 male, 60 female), and were designated as "children"; 231 subjects were more than twelve years of age (132 male, 99 female), and were designated as "adolescents." Tables 1-2 through 1-5 summarize the sample's salient characteristics.

These children and adolescents were primarily referred for evaluation by parents (36%), school officials (27%), mental health facilities (18%), and private psychiatrists (13%), while the court or family physicians initiated less than seven percent (7%) of the referrals. The sample was fairly evenly divided between Caucasian (57%) and Black (42%) children. Estimates of socioeconomic status based on education and occupation of household's

Table 1-2

Age and Sex Distribution of the Total Study Sample

Age (years)	Males n=272	Females n=159
2	1	
3	3	1
4	6	4
5	7	6
6	15	7
7	18	10
8	18	4
9	23	12
10	19	8
11	26	8
12	35	9
13	34	16
14	22	16
15	26	31
16	12	16
17	7	11
Total Sample		
Age (months) $\overline{X}$:	137.3	150.2
SD	40.5	45.2

Table 1-3

Distribution of Subject Characteristics for Male and Female Children and Adolescents

Variable and Level	Male Children n=140	Male Adolescents n=132	Female Children n=60	Female Adolescents n=99	Total N=431 n	Total N=431 %
Race						
White	74	80	32	60	246	57.0
Black	64	52	28	39	183	42.5
Latino	2				2	.5
Age Rank						
Oldest	37	37	24	37	135	31.3
Youngest	44	31	13	10	98	22.7
Only	17	14	10	8	49	11.4
Other	42	50	13	44	149	34.6
Number of Other Children in Family						
0	17	14	10	8	49	11.4
1	45	39	25	28	137	31.8
2	38	29	13	17	97	22.5
3	19	24	6	21	70	16.2
4	7	12	4	13	36	8.4
5	8	3	1	4	16	3.7
>5	6	11	1	8	26	6.0

Table 1-4

Distribution of Primary GAP Diagnoses for Male and Female Children and Adolescents

Diagnosis	Male Children n=140	Male Adolescents n=132	Female Children n=60	Female Adolescents n=99	Total N=431 n	Total N=431 %
Healthy Responses					36	8.3
Developmental Crisis	3	4		2	9	2.1
Situational Crisis	2	5	8	8	23	5.3
Other	1		3		4	.9
Reactive Disorders	18	28	7	28	81	18.8
Developmental Deviations					104	24.1
Maturational patterns	12	7	2	1	22	5.1
Motor	22	2	3		27	6.3
Speech	7		3		10	2.3
Cognitive functions	9	7	1	3	20	4.6
Social	3	8	4	1	16	3.7
Psychosexual		1		1	2	.5
Affective		1			1	.2
Integrative	2	1	2		5	1.2
Other			1		1	.2
Psychoneurotic Disorders					87	20.2
Anxiety	9	4	2	1	16	3.7
Phobic		1		2	2	.5
Conversion	1		1	1	3	.7
Dissociative				1	1	.2
Obsessive-compulsive	2				2	.5
Depressive	16	14	8	22	60	13.9
Other				3	3	.7

Table 1-4 Continued

Distribution of Primary GAP Diagnoses for Male and Female Children and Adolescents

Diagnosis	Male Children n=140	Male Adolescents n=132	Female Children n=60	Female Adolescents n=99	Total N=431 n	Total N=431 %
Personality Disorders					61	14.1
Compulsive		1			1	.2
Hysterical				1	1	.2
Anxious	3		1		4	.9
Overly dependent		4	1		5	1.2
Oppositional	1	3	1	2	7	1.6
Overly inhibited		2	1	1	4	.9
Overly independent		1		1	2	.5
Isolated		2	1		3	.7
Mistrustful	1	1			2	.5
Impulse-ridden	10	9		3	22	5.1
Neurotic	1	4		2	7	1.6
Sociosyntonic		1			1	.2
Sexual deviation		1			1	.2
Other				1	1	.2
Psychotic Disorders					17	3.9
Early infantile autism	1	1			2	.5
Other-infancy/early childhood	1				1	.2
Schizophreniform		1		2	3	.7
Other-later childhood				1	1	.2
Acute confusional state	3			1	4	.9
Schizophrenic, adult-type	2			3	5	1.2
Other				1	1	.2

	Male Children n=140	Male Adolescents n=132	Female Children n=60	Female Adolescents n=99	Total N=431 n	%
Psychophysiologic Disorders					4	.9
Gastrointestinal		1		1	2	.5
Genitourinary	1				1	.2
Other		1			1	.2
Brain Syndromes					18	4.2
Acute	1	1	1		3	.7
Chronic	6	2	6	1	15	3.5
Mental Retardation	6	2	2	1	11	2.6
Other Disorders	2	3			5	1.2
No diagnosis	1	1	1	3	6	1.4

Table 1-5

Distribution of Referral Sources for Study Sample

Referral Source	Male Children n=140	Male Adolescents n=132	Female Children n=60	Female Adolescents n=99	Total N=431 n	%
Parent	45	47	29	34	155	36.0
School	51	31	14	18	114	26.5
Mental Health Agency	21	29	7	21	78	18.1
Psychiatrist	17	13	8	16	54	12.5
Court		6	1	7	14	3.2
Family Physician	6	6	1	3	16	3.7

highest income earner (Hollingshead, 1957) placed the majority (78%) in the lowest two categories of this classification system (I=2%, II=5%, III=15%, IV=33%, V=45%).

Table 1-4 presents the distribution of primary GAP diagnoses (Group for the Advancement of Psychiatry, 1966) for the study sample. Although any subjectively applied diagnostic system may include a substantial degree of unreliability across raters, the data presented in Table 4 suggest that these subjects manifested a broad range of presenting problems, and the sample was therefore quite heterogeneous in composition. The sample was limited in the number of subjects who obtained primary diagnoses of psychosis (n=17), psychophysiologic disorders (n=4), brain syndromes (n=18) and mental retardation (n=11). Therefore, application of study results to children and adolescents who receive these classifications, should be undertaken with caution. In addition, sample restrictions may have also limited the frequency of certain criterion behaviors that might otherwise have been found to relate to PIC scales. It is possible that the limited correlates obtained for the Somatic Concern and Psychosis scales are examples of this process.

Personality Inventory for Children (PIC)

The PIC profile form is presented in Figure 1-1. The profile includes three validity, one screening, and 12 clinical scales that were constructed using one of two general methodologies. The empirical scales were constructed using the method of contrasting groups often with an additional item analytic procedure (Darlington & Bishop, 1966). Other scales were developed using a content-oriented and/or internal consistency strategy.
Validity Scales.

The scale (L) is a 15 item content scale designed to identify a tendency to deny commonly occurring behavior problems of a minor nature and to describe the child in the most virtuous of behaviors.

The F scale (F) is a 42 item scale developed to identify deviant response sets. Items comprising this scale were rarely endorsed in the normative sample ($\overline{X}$=5%).

The Defensiveness scale (DEF) is a 26 item scale constructed to measure parental defensiveness about their child's behavior. This scale was constructed using an empirical methodology.
Screening Scale.

The Adjustment scale (ADJ) was also empirically derived. This 76 item scale was contructed to identify children in need of a psychological evaluation.
Clinical Scales.

The Achievement scale (ACH) is an empirically derived 31 item scale designed to identify children with significant academic retardation.

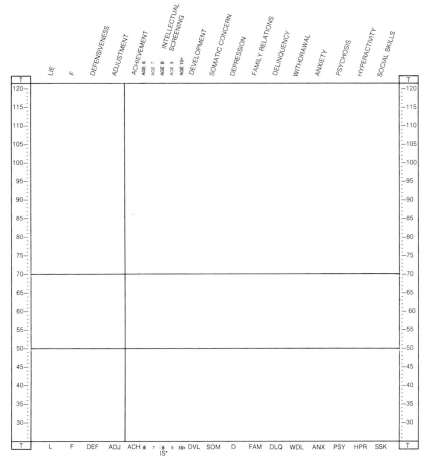

Figure 1—1
Personality Inventory for Children (PIC) Profile

The Intellectual Screening scale (IS) is a 35 item empirically constructed scale that was designed to identify impaired intellectual functioning.

The Developmental scale (DVL) is a 25 item content scale that contains items nominated by judges as measuring poor intellectual and physical development.

The Somatic Concern scale (SOM) is a 40 item scale containing items nominated by clinicians as tapping health related variables. These include: appetite, energy, strength, and frequency of and adjustment to illness.

The Depression scale (D) is a 46 item content scale. Clinicians nominated items as reflecting childhood depression.

The Family Relations scale (FAM) was constructed using a rational approach. This 35 item scale measures family effectiveness and cohesion.

The Delinquency scale (DLQ) is a 47 item scale designed to identify delinquent, antisocial tendencies. This scale was constructed using an empirical methodology.

The Withdrawal scale (WDL) is a 25 item content scale developed to measure withdrawal from social situations and preference for isolative activities.

The Anxiety scale (ANX) was developed using a rational approach. This 30 item scale encompasses the dimensions of limited frustration tolerance, irrational fears, and behavioral and psychological correlates of anxiety.

The Psychosis scale (PSY) is a 40 item empirically derived scale developed to differentiate psychotic children from normal, nonpsychotic behaviorally disturbed, and retarded children.

The Hyperactivity scale (HPR) is designed to identify children who display behavioral characteristics associated with the "hyperkinetic syndrome." This scale is comprised of 36 items and was developed using an empirical methodology.

The final clinical scale, Social Skills (SSK), is a 30 item content scale containing items nominated by judges as tapping effective social relations.

The sixteen profile scale T-scores were obtained from only those PIC protocols that were completed by female informants who had consistent contact with the child for at least the year prior to the evaluation [biological mothers (n=383), stepmothers (n=8), foster mothers (n=3), adoptive mothers (n=11), grandmothers (n=13), aunts (n=4), and female guardians (n=4)]. Protocols were scored by computer to insure scale score accuracy, and the resultant T-scores were merged with criterion data. It should be noted that no attempt was made to exclude potentially invalid test protocols on the basis of validity scale elevations, although obviously invalid protocols that reflected limited reading skills or comprehension were not included.

Readers unfamiliar with the PIC manual (Wirt et al., 1977) are urged to review this monograph in detail. Optimal application of the actuarial interpretive material presented in this volume requires an understanding of basic test philosophy, scale construction methodology, scale item composition, and scale interrelationships that are documented in this manual.

Data Analysis

The first analysis was conducted to examine the relationship between scale elevation and child age, sex, and race. This procedure was taken as a precautionary measure, although previous study had indicated that pervasive effects for sex and race were unlikely (Wirt et al., 1977, p. 43).

A three-way analysis of variance was completed to determine if any of these non-correlate demographic variables had a pervasive relationship with scale elevation. Such effects would of necessity influence the methods applied to scale correlate selection. If race, for example, was found to have a major effect on scale elevation (and this appears to be the case in adult personality inventories, cf Gynther, 1972; Gynther, Lachar, & Dahlstrom, 1978), and correlate frequencies did not differ for racial groups, a case could be made for the necessity of computing correlate-to-scale analyses separately for white and black children. Or, if adolescents received higher scores than did children on certain scales, it would be important to examine the correlates selected at the higher scale ranges to determine if these descriptors were more appropriate for adolescents.

The relationships between PIC profile scales and external criteria were examined in two stages. The first stage identified those criteria which systematically related to scale score elevation and the generalizability of this relationship across age and sex. The second stage determined the T-score ranges indicative of criterion presence or absence.

Identification of Scale Correlates. Potential scale descriptors were identified by correlational analyses. The total study sample was first divided into four sex/age subgroups: male children (n=140), female children (n=60), male adolescents (n=132), and female adolescents (n=99). Next, each of these four subgroups was randomly split, resulting in two sample groups (ns=215 and 216), each with an equal proportion of males, females, children, and adolescents. The initial statistical analysis included calculation of point biserial correlations between 322 dichotomous criteria from the three forms with each of the sixteen PIC profile scales. For each criterion to scale analysis, six correlations were computed, two for the split samples and one for each of the four sex/age groups.

The first objective of this study was to determine stable correlates, i.e., those which would generalize to a majority of behaviorally disturbed children and adolescents. Initial examination of the correlation matrices was conducted to identify *replicated* correlates for the *total sample*. All scale-criterion correlations were inspected for both split half analyses in order to identify those criteria that obtained correlations significant at $\leq$ .05 for *both* independent samples (thus resulting in a joint probability of $\leq$ .0025). This conservative level of selection reflected our concern that a great many calculations could result in several significant correlations that would reflect only chance variation. In this split sample analysis, 322 pairs of correlations were calculated for each scale. Sixteen correlations would be expected by chance to be significant at $\leq$ .05 for each scale, but only one criterion per scale would be expected by chance to receive a significant correlation for both split halves (the joint probability of both correlations being significant in independent samples = $\leq$ .0025). The generalizability of each *replicated* total sample correlate was also substantiated by inspection of the four sex/age correlations. Correlates were included as replicated if at least three of these four correlations were significant at $\leq$ .05.

The remaining scale-criterion analyses were inspected to identify two additional groups of potential correlates that demonstrated less generalizability. The first were those criteria significant at $\leq$ .01 for both age groups within the same sex, or for both sexes within the same age group. These correlates were selected because two correlations were significant at $\leq$ .01 (joint probability of significance in independent samples = $\leq$ .0001), and were descriptive of either (1) all children, (2) all adolescents, (3) all males, or (4) all females.

A final inspection of the correlation matrices was conducted for those potential criteria that had not been selected in the two previous classifications. All remaining correlates were examined to identify correlates that were significantly ($\leq$ .01) related to only one sex/age subgroup (or two, if not the same sex or same age group, such as female child, male adolescent). These correlates were only retained for further analysis when the criterion had not been previously associated with any PIC profile scale.

The last two analyses were completed to determine those correlates that might be sex or age specific, or limited in application to one sex/age group. Sex and age specific findings were investigated since significant results would not be inconsistent with the developmental psychopathology literature (cf Lapouse & Monk, 1964; Quay & Quay, 1965; Achenbach, 1966). The comprehensiveness of this analysis, in addition to reflecting our desire to determine what sort of external criteria were not systematically related to scale variation, also allowed for the definition of the construct validity dimensions for each scale. To illustrate this elaborate classification process, several examples of correlations obtained between DLQ and criteria from the psychiatric resident form are presented in Table 1-6.

Application of classification rules to Table 1-6 separates the five replicated correlates, by their sex/age correlations, into two correlates that are truly generalizable to the total sample ("Verbally hostile or argumentative," "Expresses a dislike for school"), into one correlate that is descriptive of adolescents ("History of problematic substance (drug) abuse"), into one correlate that is descriptive of children ("Previous outpatient psychotherapy"), and into one correlate that is only descriptive of female adolescents ("Precocious sexual behavior or promiscuity"). Review of the two remaining criteria placed one as a possible correlate limited to children ("Has difficulty getting to sleep"), with the other ("Teased by peers") being excluded from any further analysis.

Selection and Placement of Interpretive Descriptors. The second stage of data analysis was directed to the construction of pragmatic interpretive

Table 1-6

Examples of Classification of Criterion Scale Correlation Patterns

| Criteria | Split Sample | | Correlations with *DLQ* | | | | |
	1,n=215	2,n=216	Male Children n=140	Male Adolescents n=132	Female Children n=60	Female Adolescents n=99
Verbally hostile or argumentative	.25**	.28**	.34**	.22**	.28*	.28**
History of problematic substance (drug) abuse	.38**	.42**	ns	.42**	ns	.36**
Has difficulty getting to sleep	ns	ns	.28**	ns	.40**	ns
Teased by peers	ns	ns	ns	ns	ns	ns
Precocious sexual behavior or promiscuity	.31**	.24**	ns	ns	ns	.51**
Previous outpatient psychotherapy	.16**	.25**	.22**	ns	.22**	ns
Expresses a dislike for school	.18**	.38**	ns	.30**	.24*	.29**

ns = > .05,   * = ≤ .05,   ** = ≤ .01

guidelines for the PIC profile scales. The external criteria previously identified as scale correlates were inspected to determine those that were
unique to a given scale, or those that performed best. These correlates were
then evaluated to determine the scale elevation range that was most predictive for each correlate. Scales that were significantly related to each
criterion were listed with that criterion in decreasing order of strength of
relationship and established generalizability. For scales ACH through
SSK, the three most robust scale relationships for each correlate were
usually selected for additional study. In comparison, all replicated correlates were examined for the validity and screening scales (L through ADJ)
in the determination of these interpretive guidelines.

Unlike other personality inventories, such as the MMPI, for which scale
elevations or patterns of interpretive significance have been established by
substantial clinical experience or research application (cf Boerger, Graham & Lilly, 1974; Lachar & Alexander, 1978), it was quite possible that
a traditional rule of thumb, such as $T > 69$, might effectively predict a substantial number of criteria for one PIC scale, but be completely ineffective
for another scale. The relation between correlate presence and scale elevation was determined by tabulating criterion frequency for scale T-score
ranges. Ranges included at least 20 test protocols, and were usually 10
T-points in width, although the highest and lowest range for each scale
were larger when scale score values were infrequent. Scale elevation
ranges used to tabulate criterion frequency for total sample correlates
are presented in Table 1-7, together with the subject frequency in each
range.

Table 1-7 documents the need to evaluate each PIC profile scale separately, rather than to apply scale elevation rules uniformly. Applying a
decision rule of $> 69T$ would classify three-quarters of the study sample
for DLQ and ADJ, while classifying a quarter of the sample or less for
scales L, DEF, DVL, and FAM.

All correlate frequencies examined by scale T-score range are presented
in Appendices B and C. Although this monograph suggests application
guidelines for scale interpretation, the reader, through inspection of these
appendices, can judge the appropriateness of these decisions for any given
task. These frequency distributions could form the basis for other interpretive strategies that are tailored to meet specific programmatic goals.

The final process of determining the T-score ranges predictive of each
correlate reflected a mixture of the application of measurement theory,
assessment art, and individual preference. As will be seen, a majority of the
correlate-scale relationships examined were replicated for the total study
sample (n=400). Very few correlate-scale relationships were evaluated for
correlates with limited generalizability (n=63).

Table 1-7

Scale T-Score Ranges Used to Tabulate Criterion Frequencies

Scale		T-Score Ranges and Obtained Score Frequencies							
L	T	30-39	40-49	50-59	≥ 60				
	n	182	164	49	36				
F	T	30-59	60-69	70-79	80-89	90-99	100-109	≥ 110	
	n	60	69	81	89	45	42	45	
DEF	T	0-19	20-29	30-39	40-49	50-59	60-69	≥ 70	
	n	23	38	88	105	117	41	19	
ADJ	T	40-59	60-69	70-79	80-89	90-99	100-109	≥ 110	
	n	43	49	75	84	89	55	36	
ACH	T	20-49	50-59	60-69	70-79	≥ 80			
	n	62	119	105	90	55			
IS	T	0-39	40-49	50-59	60-69	70-79	80-89	90-109	≥ 110
	n	46	87	80	73	58	37	28	22
DVL	T	20-49	50-59	60-69	70-79	≥ 80			
	n	85	124	105	74	43			
SOM	T	30-49	50-59	60-69	70-79	80-89	≥ 90		
	n	59	86	114	81	63	28		
D	T	30-49	50-59	60-69	70-79	80-89	≥ 90		
	n	36	62	99	96	81	57		

Table 1-7 Continued
Scale T-Score Ranges Used to Tabulate Criterion Frequencies

Scale		T-Score Ranges and Obtained Score Frequencies							
FAM	T	30-49	50-59	60-69	70-79	≥80			
	n	71	124	121	84	31			
DLQ	T	30-59	60-69	70-79	80-89	90-99	100-109	110-119	≥120
	n	51	61	87	73	62	33	32	32
WDL	T	30-49	50-59	60-69	70-79	80-89	≥90		
	n	59	119	115	55	56	27		
ANX	T	30-49	50-59	60-69	70-79	80-89	≥90		
	n	49	86	138	87	51	20		
PSY	T	30-49	50-59	60-69	70-79	80-89	90-99	100-109	≥110
	n	29	69	77	70	81	47	33	25
HPR	T	20-39	40-49	50-59	60-69	70-79	≥80		
	n	51	65	78	111	60	66		
SSK	T	30-49	50-59	60-69	70-79	≥80			
	n	47	103	73	113	95			

Interpretive guidelines optimally reflect the purpose for which the interpretations are intended. If scale interpretations are to be limited to those that improve the accuracy of prediction over currently available information, or at least symptom base rates (Sechrest, 1963), the degree to which a scale can improve upon base rate prediction should be calculated. If the goal of scale interpretation is to provide accurate descriptive material, regardless of its uniqueness in the diagnostic process, correlate selection becomes the process of locating scale score ranges most *descriptive* of each criterion. The goal of this study was to provide comprehensive and accurate information based upon the PIC profile scales.

An approach that is based on maximizing correct predictions must assume the pervasive accuracy of the criteria data studied and the equal utility of correct (or incorrect) prediction of criterion presence and criterion absence. In actuality, error is introduced at both ends of the predictive process, in both the test measurement and in the criterion rating. In addition, prediction of criteria with very high or very low base rates, even when the criterion to scale score relationship is replicated and reasonably substantial, is unlikely to improve upon base rate prediction (Meehl & Rosen, 1955). Total reliance on exact criterion frequencies would limit the application of these scales' interpretations to very similar populations and would exclude infrequent or pervasive personality characteristics which are seen as important diagnostically and which have been established as stable scale correlates.

For criteria that were related to more than one of the PIC scales ACH through SSK, construction of the final scale correlate tables required determination of the primacy of scale-correlate relationships through evaluation of the relevance of criterion content. Criterion frequency and judged severity of pathology influenced the establishment of each decision rule. Other factors being equal, rules were established to lead to classifications similar to criterion base rates. Decision rules became more stringent and were applicable to a more limited proportion of the sample for those criteria that reflected severe pathology. Examples of replicated correlate frequencies by DLQ T-score ranges, and the resulting system rules, are presented in Table 1-8 to illustrate this process.

Correlate frequencies were distributed across scale T-score ranges in two general ways. In one, lower scale elevations reflected relatively equal criterion frequencies. Inspection of increasing T-score ranges usually revealed a point at which criterion frequency clearly increased, usually above base rate (see "Expresses a dislike for school", DLQ >89T). In the other distribution model, both ends of the scale score distribution are meaningful in predicting criterion absence or presence (see "Temper tantrums" DLQ < 60T, >99T; "Mother inconsistent in setting limits" DLQ< 60T, >99T).

Table 1-8

Examples of Replicated Correlate Frequencies (%) Within Scale T-Score Ranges

Replicated Correlate	BR	DLQ T-Score Ranges								Decision Rule
		30-59	60-69	70-79	80-89	90-99	100-109	110-119	≥120	
Impulsive behavior	68	40	57	61	72	76	72	84	100	>79T(55/79)
Temper tantrums	43	18	42	40	38	44	63	64	69	>99T(37/66) <60T(18/47)
Involved with the police	17	0	4	6	10	21	19	58	63	>109T(9/61)
Expresses a dislike for school	39	28	28	28	30	48	55	63	70	>89T(28/57)
Mother inconsistent in setting limits	59	27	45	61	59	64	82	89	67	>99T(52/79) <60T(27/63)

The performance of each decision rule was calculated and presented in the tables that follow after each criterion in the form of two percentages separated by a slash mark: (obtained criterion frequency below the cutting score/obtained criterion frequency above the cutting score). The notation "Temper tantrums (37/66)," for example, indicates that this criterion can be expected 37 percent of the time for children who obtain DLQ scores between 30 and 99T, while the expectation increases to 66 percent when DLQ scores exceed 99T. Correlate frequency estimates will assist the clinician in selecting report descriptors and in determining their likelihood. Phrases such as "often described," "may be indicated," or "although infrequent," can, in these instances, accurately reflect predicted correlate frequency.

The tables in Chapters 3, 4, and 5 contain replicated total sample correlates, as well as the correlates limited in generalizability by subject age or sex. The interpretive guidelines based on the most robust correlate-to-scale-relationships complete each of these tables. Scale correlates for each T-score range are presented in these tables in a set order. Those correlates unique to a given scale are presented first, in decreasing order of predicted correlate frequency, followed by correlates defined as primary and then secondary. The designation of primary versus secondary status involved several conjoint considerations: relevance of correlate content, pattern of correlates across scales, and optimal criterion classification rates. One scale was classified as primary when several scales related to the same correlate; scales classified as secondary are placed in brackets. Scale abbreviations placed in the parentheses following each correlate indicate the other scales which relate to the correlate. The final correlates in each T-score range are those which have applicability to only a portion of the study sample.

CHAPTER 2

Results-An Overview

The results of the analysis of variance for age, sex, and race effects are presented in Table 2-1. Five scales were significantly related to child sex (L, DEF, D, WDL, HPR), nine scales to child age (DEF, ACH, IS, DVL, D, DLQ, WDL, HPR, SSK), and six scales to child race (DEF, ADJ, SOM, D, ANX, SSK). Only nine of the 64 possible interactions were significant. No significant main effects or interactions were found on F, FAM, and PSY.

Previous literature has indicated that actual sex and/or age-related differences do exist (cf Lapouse & Monk, 1964; Quay & Quay, 1965; Achenbach, 1966; Werry & Quay, 1971; Gdowski, 1975). Further, Lapouse and Monk (1964) suggested that fewer differences are accounted for by race than by age or sex. Secondly, it is reasonable to assume that the nature of the presenting symptomatology influences the age at which a child would be referred for an evaluation. Externalizing acting-out behaviors, for example, are likely to lead to referrals sooner than withdrawing, internalizing symptoms (Gdowski, 1975). Finally, the fact that the informant's perception of the aversiveness of particular symptomatology is related to the age, sex, and race of the child undoubtedly accounts for a portion of the significant results. These explanations will guide the interpretation of significant effects on the profile scales.

L scale means suggested that informants were more likely to deny commonly occurring behavior problems and to ascribe virtuous behaviors when the child was female. Data has indicated that females consistently exhibited fewer behavioral difficulties (Lapouse & Monk, 1964; Werry & Quay, 1971). Means on DEF indicated that maternal defensiveness was more likely in protocols of females, adolescents, and blacks. The *Manual* (Wirt et al., 1977) indicates DEF taps denial of behavior problems. Females present with fewer difficulties, as do adolescents (Lapouse & Monk, 1964; Werry & Quay, 1971). While the race effect is unclear, it is doubtful this represents a *clinically* significant difference.

The significant three-way interaction on ADJ suggested that informants of Caucasian male ($\overline{X}$ = 86.6) and female children ($\overline{X}$ = 89.0) as well as Caucasian male adolescents ($\overline{X}$ = 91.5) described them as more psychologically maladjusted. Results on this scale are consistent with L and DEF with the exception of more ascribed pathology for Caucasian female children.

Examination of the first triad of clinical scales ACH, IS, DVL indicated a significant main effect for age. This is not an unexpected finding, as poor academic achievement and impaired cognitive functioning more frequently serve as referral foci for children. A sample selection factor undoubtedly affects adolescent T-scores, as significant impairment in these areas would have resulted in intervention and remediation earlier on in the educational experience. Thus, it is less likely that academic and/or cognitive impairment are primary in adolescents referred to a child guidance facility. The significant Sex X Age X Race interaction on ACH indicated that Caucasian female children ($\overline{X}$ = 68.7) were more likely to be referred for achievement problems, and Caucasian female adolescents ($\overline{X}$ = 58.5) were less likely to be referred for the same difficulties. Further analysis indicated a significant Age X Race effect, with cognitive impairment concerns (IS) more likely for Caucasian children ($\overline{X}$ = 69.6) and less likely for Caucasian adolescents ($\overline{X}$ = 55.6).

Analyses of clinical scales tapping internalizing behaviors (SOM, D, WDL, and ANX) indicated several main effects and interactions. Informants of blacks were more likely to view somatizing behaviors as problematic. Three-way interactions suggested that depression and anxiety-related phenomena were more likely in the descriptions of Caucasian female children [$\overline{X}$ = 78.4 (D); $\overline{X}$ = 73.9 (ANX)] and less probable for black male children [$\overline{X}$ = 64.5 (D); $\overline{X}$ = 62.2 (ANX)]. Isolative behaviors (WDL) were less problematic in Caucasian male children ($\overline{X}$ = 59.6) while more likely in the protocols of Caucasian male ($\overline{X}$ = 69.9) and black female adolescents ($\overline{X}$ = 71.7).

Scales designed to predict overt behavior difficulties (DLQ, HPR) reflected differences in age and sex. Informants of adolescents described significantly more problems with delinquent, antisocial behavior while informants of males and children were more likely to view impulsivity and dyscontrol as problematic. HPR was developed to identify children whose behavioral difficulties resemble the "hyperkinetic syndrome," and, as such, it is not unexpected that sex and age effects were reflected on this scale.

Analyses on the final clinical scale, SSK, suggested that informants of

Table 2-1

Effects of Child Sex, Age and Race on PIC Profile Scale Elevation

SCALE	Total	Sex (A) M	F	Age (B) ≤12yr	>12yr	Race (C) W	B	F ratio A	B	C	AXB	AXC	BXC	AXBXC
L	43.6	42.7	45.1	44.1	43.1	43.2	44.1	6.62**	1.99	<1	3.11	3.71	<1	<1
F	82.0	81.5	82.3	80.4	83.5	82.2	81.5	<1	2.96	<1	<1	1.81	<1	1.54
DEF	45.1	43.8	47.5	42.6	47.3	43.4	47.7	4.61*	11.42**	12.27**	1.82	<1	<1	<1
ADJ	85.5	86.2	84.3	85.0	85.9	87.8	82.2	1.35	<1	11.06**	<1	<1	<1	4.93*
ACH	63.3	64.2	62.6	65.5	62.0	63.7	63.4	<1	6.99**	<1	3.66	<1	<1	4.16*
IS	62.9	64.5	60.1	68.6	58.0	61.6	64.3	1.81	22.56**	<1	3.43	<1	4.45*	2.09
DVL	62.2	62.3	61.8	64.7	60.0	61.5	62.8	<1	11.18**	<1	2.90	<1	2.54	1.82
SOM	67.0	67.5	66.3	66.9	67.1	65.4	69.4	<1	<1	7.93**	<1	1.55	<1	<1
D	71.8	70.3	74.3	69.2	74.0	74.1	68.6	5.42*	7.81**	13.62**	3.15	<1	<1	4.47*
FAM	62.1	62.2	62.0	61.4	62.8	62.8	61.3	<1	1.16	1.63	<1	<1	<1	1.12
DLQ	84.5	83.0	86.9	76.4	91.5	85.6	83.0	<1	55.57**	<1	1.71	3.19	3.15	6.29**
WDL	65.1	63.8	67.4	62.1	67.7	65.4	64.5	4.27*	14.10**	<1	2.03	4.22*	<1	3.93*
ANX	66.0	65.5	66.7	65.8	66.2	67.7	63.9	<1	<1	8.74**	5.54*	<1	2.35	1.63
PSY	76.5	75.7	77.8	78.2	74.9	77.8	74.4	1.85	3.42	3.23	2.78	<1	<1	1.63
HPR	61.2	63.0	58.1	64.3	58.6	59.9	63.0	6.56**	9.79**	3.06	<1	<1	<1	<1
SSK	67.4	66.6	68.8	68.7	66.3	68.7	65.6	3.66	5.18*	6.49**	2.61	1.04	<1	9.62**

*p ≤ .05
**p ≤ .01

female Caucasian children ($\overline{X}$ = 76.5) were more sensitive to poor social relations, while black male adolescents ($\overline{X}$ = 61.7) were less likely to be described as such.

These analyses are generally consistent with expectations based on previous literature and sample characteristics. Of particular clinical interest is that the protocols of blacks do not appear to exaggerate problem behaviors. Higher means for blacks were only noted on DEF and SOM while significantly lower means were obtained on ADJ, D, ANX and SSK. These results are important in view of the appropriate concern that has been expressed over the accuracy of scale interpretations for minority clients based on personality assessments using the MMPI (cf Gynther, 1972).

The magnitude of the results obtained in this study are outlined in this chapter and provide a guide to the following three chapters. These chapters detail scale interpretive data separately for each criterion source. Analyses served two general objectives related to scale interpretation. The first goal was to investigate the dimensions of behavior, ability, and experience that relate to scale variance and serve to establish the construct validity of each scale. Secondly, optimal prediction of scale correlates was sought to form the basis for a comprehensive system of scale interpretation.

The first objective was sought by the identification of correlates that replicated for the total sample or were found to relate to both sexes within the same age group or both age groups for the same sex.

Table 2-2 summarizes the results of this correlational analysis. A total of 527 replicated correlates were identified, while 164 additional correlates were found that demonstrated more limited generalizability. Although PIC profile scales received an average of 33 replicated correlates and 10 additional correlates of limited applicability, the number of correlates obtained in this behaviorally disturbed sample ranged from 8 for DEF and 12 for SOM to 73 for DLQ, 72 for HPR, and 71 for ADJ. The source of these correlates also varied across scales. Parental presenting concerns were most frequently related to scales ADJ, PSY, F, SSK, DLQ, D, and ANX, and most infrequently to scales DEF, IS, SOM, FAM, and WDL. Observations made in the school environment were most often related to scales HPR, DVL, ACH, ADJ, IS, and DLQ, while few or no correlates were obtained for scales DEF, ANX, FAM, SOM, D, L, and F. Clinician impressions and observations were most often related to variation in scales DLQ, HPR, PSY, IS, ACH, ADJ, and DVL, while few correlates were obtained for scales DEF, SOM, and ANX. Variability across criterion sources was likely to reflect the differences in item content between forms as well as the degree to which an informant could accurately rate the domain in question. For example, it was clear that teachers provided

more ACH/IS/DVL correlates than parents because the school form
included more items relevant to the interpretive dimensions of these scales.
On the other hand, the very limited teacher correlates for internalizing
scales suggested that teachers were less aware of these behaviors, but were
more accurate in perceiving school performance, cognitive abilities, and
disruptive behaviors. A review of the correlates summarized in Table 2-2
revealed that 91% of the 65 parent criteria, 67% of the 95 teacher criteria,
and 56% of the 162 clinician criteria obtained stable correlations with
one or more PIC profile scale.

Table 2-2

Summary of PIC Profile Scale Correlates Derived from Three Sources

SCALE	Parent	Teacher	Clinician	Total
L	15 (5) [a]	0 (2)	7 (5)	22 (12)
F	22 (6)	0 (4)	6 (2)	28 (12)
DEF	4 (4)	0 (0)	0 (0)	4 (4)
ADJ	30 (3)	10 (9)	13 (6)	53 (18)
ACH	12 (5)	19 (6)	19 (1)	50 (12)
IS	6 (3)	15 (4)	17 (4)	38 (11)
DVL	12 (6)	23 (2)	16 (3)	51 (11)
SOM	6 (3)	0 (0)	1 (2)	7 (5)
D	22 (1)	0 (2)	5 (4)	27 (7)
FAM	7 (3)	0 (0)	7 (3)	14 (6)
DLQ	20 (4)	14 (5)	22 (8)	56 (17)
WDL	8 (3)	2 (2)	3 (6)	13 (11)
ANX	21 (1)	0 (0)	3 (1)	24 (2)
PSY	23 (10)	2 (3)	18 (4)	43 (17)
HPR	17 (3)	24 (2)	21 (5)	62 (10)
SSK	20 (5)	5 (2)	10 (2)	35 (9)
TOTAL	245 (65)	114 (43)	168 (56)	527 (164)

[a]Indicates the number of correlates significant for both sexes in the same age group
or both ages for the same sex.

Another source of apparent poor performance of a limited number of
profile scales was the nature of the study sample. The majority of the evaluations can be characterized as assessments of child behavior problems
initiated by parents. Within this context, the lack of a substantial number
of correlates for the Defensiveness scale can be attributed to the restricted
range of DEF. Review of the PIC manual (Wirt et al., 1977) indicates that
the criterion "high-defensive" mothers usually produced a DEF scale score
of $\geq$ 69T. In our sample only 5% of the PIC profiles fell within this range.

Table 2-3

Frequency of Scale Correlate Placements Selected from Three Sources

PIC SCALE	<40T			<50T			<60T			>49T			>59T			>69T			>79T			>89T			>99T			>109T			>119T		
	P	T	C*	P	T	C	P	T	C	P	T	C	P	T	C	P	T	C	P	T	C	P	T	C	P	T	C	P	T	C	P	T	C
L										4	3		8	2																			
F							2						1			1						5	2		2	2		2	1				
DEF																																	
ADJ							5	1											3			3	2	5	12	3	3	4	1				
ACH				2	3	2							3	8		2	5	8	2	7	9												
IS	2												5			2	3	3	1	3	6	2	7	6									
DVL				2	9	2							3	11	2	6	11		5	6	2							2					
SOM				3												2	2		1	2													
D				6	1											8	5		4	3													
FAM	1												2						1			1											
DLQ							7	5	10				2			1			11	7	6	1	3	3	1	1	8	3	1	8	1		
WDL				1	1											1	1	1	2	2													
ANX				6	1								1			7	1		5	1													
PSY				1	4		9									2			6	1		3	2	6	4	1	3						
HPR	3	8	7	2	3								14	15	9	2	9	10	1	1								3	3	5			
SSK				6	3	3							3			5	1	4	1	3	1												

*P = parent, T = teacher, C = clinician

The poor performance of SOM cannot be attributed to a restricted score range, as 40% of the SOM values exceeded 69T, but instead may reflect in this sample limited potential somatizing correlates and idiosyncratic sample characteristics as well as a general emphasis of informants on overt behavior. The potential for this scale might best be determined in a pediatric psychology population where various components of somatization are often included in the presenting complaints. The relatively poor performance of PSY clearly reflected the infrequency of psychotic behaviors in the study sample.

Table 2-2 facilitates the comparison of the relative robustness of empirically constructed scales to those constructed using a content/internal consistency approach. Although the latter approach has proven of value in adult personality assessment (Lachar & Alexander, 1978), the empirically keyed scales in ACH through SSK clearly were the best performers. The interpretation of the significance of this observation is difficult, however, as three of the empirically keyed scales represent the most salient dimensions in this sample: behavior dyscontrol and poor academic achievement (ACH, DLQ, HPR) (Lachar & Gdowski, 1979).

The second goal of this study was to determine the optimal prediction of potential scale correlates in order to form the basis for a comprehensive system of scale interpretation. Table 2-3 provides a summary of this process and indicates the optimal scale T-score ranges in which correlates were obtained. This table does not include those limited scale correlates applicable to only one sex/age sample. If these are included (see Appendix C), 92% of parent criteria, 72% of teacher criteria, and 64% of clinician generated criteria are predicted by one or more PIC profile scale. The final analyses included 232 different correlates examined within 428 scale-criteria correlations.

Table 2-3 suggests that the range of clinically significant T-scores is not consistent across PIC profile scales. The following ranges, and the percent of study protocols classified, were initially suggested by this data for interpretation of the PIC profile scales:

>49T: L (20%)
>59T: DEF (14%), ACH (58%), IS (51%), DVL (52%), FAM (54%), HPR (55%)
>69T: SOM (40%), D (54%), WDL (32%), ANX (36%), SSK (47%)
>79T: DLQ (46%), PSY (37%)
>89T: F (31%), ADJ (42%)

CHAPTER 3

Presenting Complaints and Parental Concerns

This chapter documents the relation between parental observation and recall of developmental milestones, current behavior problems, and the PIC profile scales. Although some readers may be inclined to minimize the importance of these data, as the same informant generated both the criteria and PIC scores, this potential criticism may be attenuated by several considerations.

First, the parental observations were obtained within the context of application for evaluation of their child, usually several weeks before the PIC was completed. Parents had the advantage of consulting with other family members and baby books in completing this application form which was then compared to PIC scale scores obtained solely from the responses of the child's mother. A fact that is hard to overlook is the qualitative and economic superiority of a mother's observation and "understanding" of her child, compared to other sources of information. This superiority need not be minimized because the mother is also the source of test responses. Not only do parents routinely serve as the sole source of developmental data and structure the dimensions of child behavior that they find troublesome, but the data thereby generated can serve to highlight the meaning of PIC scores by indicating those scale ranges predictive of these concerns and observations.

Hindsight has suggested that our initial concern for minimizing the effort needed to complete each criterion form may have led to an unnecessary simplicity in item content and a resulting loss of useful information. It is our hope that other investigators will elaborate on our results by gathering more highly differentiated correlates.

The scales are presented in the order in which they appear on the PIC profile. Scale correlates are followed by those selected in the manner as described in Chapter I to form an interpretive guide.

Table 3-1

Lie Scale (L): Presenting Complaints and Parental Concerns

Total Sample:

Disobeys parents   (-.41, -.33)
Can't be trusted   (-.34, -.30)
Steals   (-.28, -.28)
Won't obey school rules   (-.32, -.26)
Lies   (-.37, -.25)
Poor loser   (-.31, -.25)
Talks back to grown-ups   (-.36, -.24)
Breaks things   (-.24, -.23)
Picks on other children   (-.32, -.23)
Fights with other children   (-.38, -.21)
Has temper tantrums   (-.25, -.17)
Doesn't finish things (short attention span)   (-.26, -.16)
Demands too much attention   (-.26, -.15)
Has a "chip on the shoulder"   (-.31, -.15)
Acts without thinking   (-.39, -.11)

Adolescents Only:	**Male**	**Female**
Has problems learning in school	-.28	-.24
Often skips school	-.26	-.33
Hangs around with a "bad crowd"	-.28	-.25
Runs away from home	-.20	-.25
Acts younger than real age	-.21	-.23

Correlate Placement:

>59T (L)* Acts without thinking (75/40) (ADJ)
     (L)   Lies (65/29)
     (L)   Has temper tantrums (59/36) (F, ADJ)
     (L)   Demands too much attention(57/34)
     (L)   Poor loser (56/28) (DEF)
     (L)   Fights with other children (52/17) (ADJ)
     (L)   Breaks things (42/11) (F, ADJ)
     (L)   Runs away from home (35/5) (F)

>49T (L)   Disobeys parents (74/33) (F, ADJ)
     (L)   Can't be trusted (59/25) (F, ADJ)
     (L)   Often skips school (47/16) (ADJ)
     (L)   Hangs around with a "bad crowd" (44/16)

*Scale range suggests reduced frequency of correlate.

Minimal elevation of L suggests a greatly diminished probability of the presence of symptoms of hostility and dyscontrol which could serve to motivate parents to seek professional assistance. All significant criteria were inversely related to scale elevation.

Table 3-2

F Scale (F): Presenting Complaints and Parental Concerns

Total Sample:

Says or does strange or peculiar things   (.38, .28)
Can't be trusted   (.29, .27)
Trouble falling asleep   (.34, .27)
Plays alone most of the time   (.27, .26)
Breaks things   (.24, .29)
Refuses to go to bed   (.34, .22)
Tired most of the time   (.22, .29)
Has few or no friends   (.28, .21)
Has temper tantrums   (.25, .20)
Is sad or unhappy much of the time   (.19, .23)
Has a "chip on the shoulder"   (.18, .23)
Mood changes quickly or without reason   (.20, .17)
Runs away from home   (.17, .19)
Disobeys parents   (.17, .27)
Steals   (.16, .26)
Lies   (.15, .27)
Clumsy or accident prone   (.15, .22)
Won't obey school rules   (.15, .20)
Picks on other children   (.14, .23)
Is often confused or in a daze   (.30, .13)
Doesn't trust other people   (.12, .30)
Can't sit still   (.11, .18)

	Child	Adolescent
Females Only:		
Slow to first walk by self	.42	.33
Fights with other children	.37	.23
Talks back to grown-ups	.36	.26
Males Only:		
Has sex play with other children	.22	.24
Wakes up very early	.27	.20

	Male	Female
Adolescents Only:		
Acts younger than real age	.23	.23

Correlate Placement:

>109T   Trouble falling asleep (28/67)
     Is often confused or in a daze (37/60) (ADJ)

> 99T   Breaks things (34/62) (L, ADJ)
     Refuses to go to bed (24/51)

> 89T   Has temper tantrums (50/73) (L, ADJ)
     Can't be trusted (44/69) (L, ADJ)
     Has few or no friends (43/64) (ADJ)
     Says or does strange or peculiar things (34/61)
     Runs away from home (17/29) (L)

Table 3-2 Continued (F)
Correlate Placement:
> 69T Disobeys parents (48/74) (L, ADJ)
< 60T (L)* Trouble falling asleep (28/67)
     (L)   Says or does strange or peculiar things (34/61)

---

*Scale range suggests reduced frequency of correlate.

Aside from identification of atypical response sets (see Wirt et al., 1977, pp. 50-52), F scale elevation in excess of 89T reflects a variety of externalizing and internalizing presenting complaints. The majority of the final correlates are also characteristic of the Adjustment Scale (ADJ).

Table 3-3

Defensiveness Scale (DEF): Presenting Complaints and Parental Concerns

---

Total Sample:
    Fights with other children   (-.29, -.25)
    Wants things to be perfect   (-.25, -.16)
    Poor loser   (-.18, -.16)
    Disobeys parents (-.14, -.16)

Males Only:	**Child**	**Adolescent**
Picks on other children	-.34	-.25
Lies	-.19	-.24
Demands too much attention	-.21	-.29
Can't sit still	-.29	-.21

DEF, like L, was consistently found to be inversely related to the presence of parental concern over child behaviors characterized by hostility and dyscontrol. The current data do not contribute substantially beyond the PIC manual to the application of this scale.

Table 3-4

Adjustment Scale (ADJ): Presenting Complaints and Parental Concerns

---

Total Sample:
    Has few or no friends   (.37, .39)
    Can't be trusted   (.34, .40)
    Disobeys parents   (.32, .39)
    Plays alone most of the time   (.34, .31)
    Won't obey school rules   (.29, .33)
    Has problems learning in school   (.31, .27)
    Can't sit still   (.31, .27)

Table 3-4 Continued (ADJ)
Total Sample:

Acts without thinking (.28, .26)
Breaks things (.38, .26)
Doesn't finish things (short attention span) (.37, .25)
Steals (.25, .32)
Fights with other children (.25, .29)
Talks back to grown-ups (.25, .31)
Says or does strange or peculiar things (.39, .24)
Has a "chip on the shoulder" (.23, .24)
Lies (.29, .22)
Is often confused or in a daze (.28, .21)
Refuses to go to bed (.28, .21)
Trouble falling asleep (.30, .21)
Has temper tantrums (.32, .20)
Acts younger than real age (.26, .20)
Clumsy or accident prone (.19, .27)
Has sex play with other children (.19, .29)
Is sad or unhappy much of the time (.24, .19)
Picks on other children (.18, .27)
Slow to become completely toilet trained (.19, .17)
Demands too much attention (.23, .17)
Hurts self on purpose (.20, .17)
Slow to first walk by self (.15, .27)
Mood changes quickly or without reason (.33, .13)

Adolescents Only:	**Male**	**Female**
Not fully toilet trained (wets bed, soils, etc.)	.23	.23
Often skips school	.23	.25

Females Only:	**Child**	**Adolescent**
Slow to first stand alone	.40	.23

Correlate Placement:

>109T Often skips school (38/79) (L)
Is often confused or in a daze (37/69) (F)
Has sex play with other children (12/36)
Hurts self on purpose (13/31)

>99T Acts without thinking (67/91) (L)
Doesn't finish things (short attention span) (65/90)
Can't be trusted (44/82) (L, F)
Talks back to grown-ups (52/79)
Has temper tantrums (52/76) (L, F)
Fights with other children (43/74) (L)
Plays alone most of the time (37/69)
Breaks things (33/65) (L, F)
Steals (29/59)
Clumsy or accident prone (32/54)
Slow to first walk by self (8/25)
Slow to become completely toilet trained (7/21)

Table 3-4 Continued (ADJ)
Corrleate Plecement:
> 89T Disobeys parents (54/83) (L, F)
        Has problems learning in school (51/75)
        Has few or no friends (37/67)

< 60T (L)* Is often confused or in a daze (37/69)
        (L)   Plays alone most of the time (37/69)
        (L)   Has few or no friends (37/67)
        (L)   Steals (29/59)
        (L)   Clumsy or accident prone (32/54)

---

*Scale range suggests reduced frequency of correlate.

ADJ, beyond identifying children with problems that warrant psychological evaluation, accurately reflects the broad scope of concerns which motivate parents to seek assistance. These data also suggest that increasing ADJ elevation reflects both increasing variety and frequency of problem behaviors.

Table 3-5

Achievement Scale (ACH): Presenting Complaints and Parental Concerns

Total Sample:
        Has problems learning in school   (.50, .42)
        Acts younger than real age   (.41, .29)
        Breaks things   (.34, .25)
        Can't sit still   (.25, .29)
        Acts without thinking   (.25, .25)
        Plays alone most of the time   (.25, .24)
        Doesn't finish things (short attention span)   (.33, .23)
        Doesn't speak well   (.23, .26)
        Is often confused or in a daze   (.26, .19)
        Slow to first walk by self   (.18, .30)
        Has few or no friends   (.15, .21)
        Says or does strange or peculiar things   (.31, .13)

Children Only:	**Male**	**Female**
Slow to speak first real sentences	.19	.27

Females Only:	**Child**	**Adolescent**
Picks on other children	.31	.27
Slow to toilet train	.24	.23

Adolescents Only:	**Male**	**Female**
Disobeys parents	.23	.31
Can't be trusted	.20	.23

Table 3-5 Continued (ACH)
Correlate Placement:

>79T [Slow to first walk by self (7/38)] (DVL, PSY)
      [Doesn't speak well (15/43)] (IS, DVL)

> 69T Has problems learning in school (49/86) (IS, DVL)
      [Breaks things (30/58)] (DLQ, PSY, HPR, SSK)

> 59T [Doesn't finish things (short attention span) (58/80)] (DVL, HPR)
      [Acts younger than real age (26/59)] (IS, DVL, PSY)
      [Is often confused or in a daze (28/48)] (PSY)

< 50T (L)* Has problems learning in school (23/68) (DVL)
  (L) [Breaks things (18/43)] (DLQ, PSY, HPR, SSK)

---

*Scale range suggests reduced frequency of correlate.

ACH clearly reflects parental concern over academic achievement as well as suggests some of the causes and sequelae of academic retardation.

Table 3-6

Intellectual Screening Scale (IS): Presenting Complaints and Parental Concerns

---

Total Sample:
     Acts younger than real age   (.29, .34)
     Has problems learning in school   (.31, .25)
     Doesn't speak well   (.23, .28)
     Slow to speak first real sentences   (.19, .26)
     Says or does strange or peculiar things   (.19, .16)
     Slow to first dress self   (.16, .23)

Children Only:	**Male**	**Female**
Slow to first sit up	.20	.50
Slow to first walk by self	.26	.45

Adolescents Only:	**Male**	**Female**
Plays alone most of the time	.19	.28

Correlate Placement:

>89T Slow to speak first real sentences (17/42)
     Slow to first dress self (6/22)

> 79T Acts younger than real age (38/74) (ACH, DVL, PSY)

> 69T [Has problems learning in school (47/75)] (ACH, DVL)
     [Doesn't speak well (13/30)] (ACH, DVL)

The parental concern "Acts younger than real age" accurately reflects the function of IS as well as documents parents' accurate perception of retarded physical and social development.

Table 3-7

Development Scale (DVL): Presenting Complaints and Parental Concerns

Total Sample:
    Has problems learning in school   (.52, .39)
    Acts younger than real age   (.44, .30)
    Doesn't finish things (short attention span)   (.34, .28)
    Breaks things   (.32, .22)
    Can't sit still   (.21, .30)
    Doesn't speak well   (.21, .26)
    Acts without thinking   (.21, .26)
    Plays alone most of the time   (.21, .24)
    Slow to first stand alone   (.19, .23)
    Is often confused or in a daze   (.23, .17)
    Slow to first walk by self   (.13, .37)
    Slow to speak first real words   (.13, .23)

Adolescents Only:	**Male**	**Female**
Not fully toilet trained (wets bed, soils, etc.)	.22	.24
Disobeys parents	.21	.32

Females Only:	**Child**	**Adolescent**
Slow to first dress self	.35	.23
Picks on other children	.31	.26
Has few or no friends	.28	.34
Clumsy or accident prone	.31	.23

Correlate Placement:
>79T Slow to speak first real words (21/49) (PSY)
         Slow to first walk by self (8/42) (ACH, PSY)
         Doesn't speak well (16/40) (ACH, IS)
         Slow to first stand alone (4/21) (PSY)
         Not fully toilet trained (wets bed, soils, etc.) (11/42)
            [Adolescents only]

>59T [Has problems learning in school (40/81)] (ACH, IS)
         [Doesn't finish things (short attention span) (60/80)] (ACH, HPR)
         [Acts younger than real age (29/61)] (ACH, IS, PSY)

<50T (L)* Acts younger than real age (23/51) (PSY)
         (L) [Has problems learning in school (22/71)] (ACH)

---

*Scale range suggests reduced frequency of correlate.

DVL reflects developmental delay in physical maturation and verbal ability, even when delay is classified by conservative standards. DVL correlates also reflect the effects of these developmental deviations.

Table 3-8

Somatic Concern Scale (SOM): Presenting Complaints and Parental Concerns

Total Sample:

Tired most of the time   (.26, .33)
Has aches and pains   (.38, .20)
Fakes being sick   (.27, .20)
Trouble falling asleep   (.18, .19)
Says or does strange or peculiar things   (.19, .16)
Is often confused or in a daze   (.24, .14)

Males Only:	**Child**	**Adolescent**
During pregnancy mother had severe emotional problems	.19	.31
Wakes up very early	.24	.26
Demands too much attention	.21	.22

Correlate Placement:

>79T Tired most of the time (22/51)

>69T Has aches and pains (27/54) (D, ANX)
       Fakes being sick (18/41) (ANX)

<50T (L)* Tired most of the time (14/31)
       (L)   Fakes being sick (14/29)
       (L)   [Has aches and pains (20/40)] (D, ANX)

---

*Scale range suggests reduced frequency of correlate.

SOM clearly relates at the traditional level of "clinical significance" (>69T) to somatization phenomenon. The three potential parent correlates that reflect somatization were the three strongest replicated SOM correlates from the parent application form.

Table 3-9

Depression Scale (D): Presenting Complaints and Parental Concerns

Total Sample:

Is sad or unhappy much of the time   (.47, .53)
Plays alone most of the time   (.42, .48)
Has few or no friends   (.42, .44)
Afraid of many things   (.33, .32)
Cries a lot   (.36, .30)
Has aches and pains   (.33, .28)
Trouble falling asleep   (.27, .31)
Tired most of the time   (.26, .36)
Very shy   (.25, .26)

Table 3-9 Continued (D)
Total Sample:
> Doesn't trust other people   (.22, .44)
> Doesn't eat right   (.29, .21)
> Wants things to be perfect   (.27, .21)
> Mood changes quickly or without reason   (.33, .20)
> Is afraid to go to school   (.32, .19)
> Refuses to go to bed   (.19, .21)
> Is often confused or in a daze   (.19, .21)
> Says or does strange or peculiar things   (.21, .18)
> Acts younger than real age   (.18, .19)
> Has temper tantrums   (.16, .16)
> Demands too much attention   (.15, .14)
> Talks back to grown-ups   (.12, .24)
> Is picked on by other children   (.12, .23)

Adolescents Only:	Male	Female
Fakes being sick	.22	.29

Correlate Placement:
>89T [Is afraid to go to school (15/39)] (WDL, ANX, SSK)
> Has threatened or attempted suicide (26/44)
> [Male adolescents only]

>79T Doesn't eat right (19/42) (ANX)
> Refuses to go to bed (24/42) (PSY)
> [Plays alone most of the time (30/73)] (WDL, PSY, SSK)
> [Afraid of many things (19/43)] (ANX)
> Hurts self on purpose (5/20) [Male adolescents only]

>69T Mood changes quickly or without reason (53/76)
> Is sad or unhappy much of the time (29/73) (ANX)
> Cries a lot (21/50) (ANX, PSY)
> [Has few or no friends (29/67)] (PSY, SSK)
> [Has aches and pains (25/48)] (SOM, ANX)
> [Trouble falling asleep (18/45)] (ANX, PSY)
> [Doesn't trust other people (15/45)] (ANX)
> [Wants things to be perfect (22/44)] (ANX)

<50T (L)* Afraid of many things (0/29)
> (L)   Is sad or unhappy much of the time (3/57) (ANX)
> (L)   Cries a lot (8/39) (ANX)
> (L)   [Has aches and pains (8/40)] (SOM, ANX)
> (L)   [Has few or no friends (11/53)] (PSY, SSK)
> (L)   [Trouble falling asleep (14/34)] (ANX, PSY)

---

*Scale range suggests reduced frequency of correlate.

D elevations exceeding 69T clearly reflect parental concern over child unhappiness. D correlates reflect sadness and the varied symptomatology with which it is frequently associated.

Table 3-10

Family Relations Scale (FAM): Presenting Complaints and Parental Concerns

Total Sample:		
Trouble falling asleep (.21, .21)		
Doesn't trust other people (.23, .20)		
Disobeys parents (.20, .21)		
Is sad or unhappy much of the time (.16, .17)		
Fakes being sick (.23, .15)		
Refuses to go to bed (.22, .15)		
Can't sit still (.14, .20)		
Children Only:	**Male**	**Female**
During pregnancy mother had severe emotional problems	.22	.27
Adolescents Only:		
Often skips school	.19	.27
Males Only:	**Child**	**Adolescent**
Demands too much attention	.23	.29

The analysis presented in Table 3-10 may be interpreted as documenting the effect of family and parental conflict on children. Correlates reflecting parental and family characteristics (except for "During pregnancy mother had severe emotional problems") are absent in this analysis because these items were only placed on the form completed by clinicians. No interpretive guidelines were generated by this analysis.

Table 3-11

Delinquency Scale (DLQ): Presenting Complaints and Parental Concerns

Total Sample:
Often skips school   (.60, .51)
Hangs around with a "bad crowd"   (.50, .48)
Disobeys parents   (.46, .43)
Can't be trusted   (.45, .43)
Steals   (.43, .43)
Uses drugs   (.39, .42)
Runs away from home   (.48, .37)
Won't obey school rules   (.37, .47)
Talks back to grown-ups   (.37, .41)
Has a "chip on the shoulder"   (.42, .34)
Lies   (.39, .33)
Has temper tantrums   (.30, .29)
Has sex play with other children   (.23, .22)

Table 3-11 Continued (DLQ)
Total Sample:
       Fights with other children   (.23, .22)
       Trouble falling asleep   (.20, .17)
       Breaks things   (.19, .17)
       Picks on other children   (.17, .18)
       Refuses to go to bed   (.13, .18)
       Acts without thinking   (.25, .12)
       Says or does strange or peculiar things   (.22, .13)

Children Only:	**Male**	**Female**
Has few or no friends	.26	.38
Plays alone most of the time	.22	.36
Mood changes quickly or without reason	.37	.53

Males Only:	**Child**	**Adolescent**
Can't sit still	.22	.32

Correlate Placement:

>109T Often skips school (16/79)
      Runs away from home (14/59)
      Uses drugs (7/43)

> 99T Has sex play with other children (10/28)

> 89T Hangs around with a "bad crowd" (13/52)

> 79T Has a "chip on the shoulder" (31/64)
      Disobeys parents (45/84) (HPR)
      Lies (43/78) (HPR)
      Talks back to grown-ups (38/74) (HPR)
      Won't obey school rules (37/74) (HPR)
      Can't be trusted (30/71) (HPR)
      Steals (15/53) (HPR)
      [Has temper tantrums (41/71)] (PSY, SSK)
      [Fights with other children (36/61)] (HPR, SSK)
      [Picks on other children (31/51)] (HPR, SSK)
      [Breaks things (29/49)] (ACH, PSY, HPR, SSK)

< 60T (L)* Often skips school (0/28)
      (L)   Talks back to grown-ups (14/64)
      (L)   Has a "chip on the shoulder" (16/53)
      (L)   Disobeys parents (18/72)
      (L)   Has temper tantrums (22/62)
      (L)   [Breaks things (14/43)] (ACH, PSY, HPR, SSK)
      (L)   [Won't obey school rules (22/61)] (HPR)

---

*Scale range suggests reduced frequency of correlate.

DLQ reflects parental concern over child behavior characterized as hostile and antisocial. DLQ elevations in excess of 79T are strongly suggestive of a disregard for societal limits. Table 3-11 suggests that increasing elevations reflect more deviant behaviors.

Table 3-12

Withdrawal Scale (WDL): Presenting Complaints and Parental Concerns

Total Sample:

  Plays alone most of the time   (.42, .35)
  Is sad or unhappy much of the time   (.33, .32)
  Very shy   (.47, .31)
  Has few or no friends   (.35, .27)
  Tired most of the time   (.24, .23)
  Afraid of many things   (.24, .22)
  Is afraid to go to school   (.29, .20)
  Acts younger than real age   (.16, .15)

	Child	Adolescent
Females Only:		
Slow to first walk by self	.29	.25
Males Only:		
Trouble falling asleep	.21	.32
Is often confused or in a daze	.29	.24

Correlate Placement:

>79T Very shy (17/61) (ANX)
      [Is afraid to go to school (15/33)] (D, ANX, SSK)

>69T [Plays alone most of the time (33/67)] (D, PSY, SSK)

<50T (L)* [Plays alone most of the time (19/48)] (PSY, SSK)

---

*Scale range suggests reduced frequency of correlate.

WDL reflects the limited dimension of social withdrawal. Scale correlates suggest that WDL elevation may be causally related to other internalizing symptoms, such as depression or anxiety. These data also suggest that WDL elevation is often accompanied by elevation of SSK, WDL reflecting one of several possible causes for limited social skills and satisfying relationships.

Table 3-13

Anxiety Scale (ANX): Presenting Complaints and Parental Concerns

Total Sample:

  Afraid of many things   (.44, .43)
  Is sad or unhappy much of the time   (.40, .41)
  Has few or no friends   (.35, .37)
  Plays alone most of the time   (.27, .38)
  Doesn't trust other people   (.24, .36)

Table 3-13 Continued (ANX)
Total Sample:

      Trouble falling asleep (.24, .28)
      Has aches and pains (.35, .23)
      Cries a lot (.40, .22)
      Tired most of the time (.22, .26)
      Demands too much attention (.21, .22)
      Nightmares (.24, .20)
      Is picked on by other children (.20, .23)
      Very shy (.20, .31)
      Wants things to be perfect (.30, .20)
      Is afraid to go to school (.30, 19)
      Doesn't eat right (.21, .19)
      Refuses to go to bed (.17, .21))
      Has a "chip on the shoulder" (.17, .21)
      Fakes being sick (.23, .16)
      Has temper tantrums (.17, .14)
      Mood changes quickly or without reason (.21, .13)

Adolescents Only:	**Male**	**Female**
Is often confused or in a daze	.22	.29

Correlate Placement:

>79T Nightmares (22/46)
      Wants things to be perfect (30/57) (D)
      Is afraid to go to school (15/34) (D, WDL, SSK)
      [Has aches and pains (33/60)] (SOM, D)
      [Fakes being sick (25/41)] (SOM)

>69T Doesn't trust other people (22/47) (D)
      Afraid of many things (15/46) (D)
      Trouble falling asleep (25/45) (D, PSY)
      [Is sad or unhappy much of the time (41/73)] (D)
      [Cries a lot (28/52)] (D, PSY)
      [Very shy (19/38)] (WDL)
      [Doesn't eat right (21/36)] (D)

>59T [Demands too much attention (45/60)] (SSK)

<50T (L)* Very shy (10/28)
      (L) Doesn't trust other people (10/34)
      (L) Has aches and pains (8/41) (SOM, D)
      (L) Trouble falling asleep (14/35) (D, PSY)
      (L) [Cries a lot (10/40)] (D)
      (L) [Is sad or unhappy much of the time (17/57)] (D)

---

*Scale range suggests reduced frequency of correlate.

ANX elevation reflects parental concern about child fearfulness and worry. Such discomfort is often associated with symptoms of depression and somatization.

Table 3-14

Psychosis Scale (PSY): Presenting Complaints and Parental Concerns

Total Sample:

Plays alone most of the time   (.51, .45)
Has few or no friends   (.44, .38)
Says or does strange or peculiar things   (.34, .30)
Trouble falling asleep   (.29, .27)
Refuses to go to bed   (.25, .31)
Acts younger than real age   (.27, .25)
Cries a lot   (.28, .23)
Breaks things   (.22, .27)
Slow to first walk by self   (.21, .22)
Slow to toilet train   (.24, .20)
Demands too much attention   (.22, .20)
Doesn't finish things (short attention span)   (.28, .20)
Is picked on by other children   (.19, .24)
Is often confused or in a daze   (.34, .18)
Slow to first stand alone   (.18, .20)
Has temper tantrums   (.17, .22)
Clumsy or accident prone   (.16, .21)
Daydreams a lot   (.27, .15)
Is sad or unhappy much of the time   (.15, .19)
Doesn't speak well   (.14, .24)
Very shy   (.25, .13)
Fakes being sick   (.20, .13)
Slow to speak first real sentences   (.12, .24)

Females Only:	**Child**	**Adolescent**
Slow to first sit up	.52	.27
Slow to first crawl	.47	.22
Slow to first dress self	.43	.31
Fights with other children	.33	.28
Talks back to grown-ups	.32	.25
Males Only:		
Tired most of the time	.20	.29
Afraid of many things	.19	.34
Adolescents Only:	**Male**	**Female**
Not fully toilet trained (wets bed, soils, etc.)	.20	.24
Fakes being sick	.22	.27
Children Only:		
Mood changes quickly or without reason	.25	.41

Correlate Placement:
>109T [Slow to first walk by self (10/40)] (ACH, DVL)
     Slow to first sit up (7/67) [Females only]
     Slow to first crawl (10/67) [Females only]

Table 3-14 Continued (PSY)
Correlate Placement:

> 99T Slow to toilet train (8/24)
        [Refuses to go to bed (25/60)] (D)
        [Slow to speak first real words (17/34)] (DVL)
        [Slow to first stand alone (4/16)] (DVL)

> 89T [Acts younger than real age (39/65)] (ACH, IS, DVL)
        [Breaks things (33/60)] (ACH, DLQ, HPR, SSK)
        [Trouble falling asleep (27/50)] (D, ANX)

> 79T Says or does strange or peculiar things (31/58)
        Daydreams a lot (33/52)
        Has temper tantrums (50/66) (DLQ, SSK)
        Is picked on by other children (39/60) (ANX, SSK)
        Is often confused or in a daze (30/52) (ACH)
        [Cries a lot (27/50)] (ANX)

> 69T [Has few or no friends (25/66)] (D, SSK)
        [Plays alone most of the time (15/64)] (D, WDL, SSK)

< 60T (L)* Says or does strange or peculiar things (21/49)
        (L)   Daydreams a lot (22/47)

< 50T (L)   Is often confused or in a daze (3/42)
        (L)   Refuses to go to bed (14/31)
        (L)   [Has few or no friends (7/53)] (D, SSK)
        (L)   [Plays alone most of the time (7/47)] (WDL, SSK)
        (L)   [Trouble falling asleep (10/34)] (D, ANX)
        (L)   [Acts younger than real age (17/47)] (DVL)
        (L)   [Breaks things (17/41)] (ACH, DLQ, HPR, SSK)

---

*Scale range suggests reduced frequency of correlate

In this primarily nonpsychotic sample, PSY >79T suggests behavior judged as being "strange or peculiar," cognitive confusion, and withdrawal or preoccupation. Higher PSY elevations suggest parental concern over immaturity and impaired development. PSY >99T can reflect either poor reality testing and/or developmental retardation.

Table 3-15

Hyperactivity Scale (HPR): Presenting Complaints and Parental Concerns

---

Total Sample:
        Can't sit still   (.50, .50)
        Won't obey school rules   (.49, .45)
        Fights with other children   (.49, .43)

Table 3-15 Continued (HPR)
Total Sample:

Picks on other children   (.45, .41)
Acts without thinking   (.42, .35)
Poor loser   (.31, .30)
Can't be trusted   (.36, .29)
Very shy   (-.29, -.29)
Breaks things   (.32, .28)
Steals   (.33, .27)
Talks back to grown-ups   (.29, .27)
Disobeys parents   (.24, .28)
Clumsy or accident prone   (.29, .22)
Doesn't finish things (short attention span)   (.34, .21)
Lies   (.42, .20)
Has a "chip on the shoulder"   (.27, .17)
Has sex play with other children   (.13, .20)

Males Only:	**Child**	**Adolescent**
Sets fires	.27	.28

Adolescents Only:	**Male**	**Female**
Demands too much attention	.37	.24
Hangs around with a "bad crowd"	.36	.24

Correlate Placement:

>69T Sets fires (9/26)
        [Steals (26/58)] (DLQ)

>59T Acts without thinking (54/86)
        Can't sit still (33/83)
        Poor loser (38/66)
        Clumsy or accident prone (24/47)
        (L)* Very shy (37/17)
        Doesn't finish things (short attention span) (56/82) (ACH, DVL)
        Fights with other children (27/67) (DLQ, SSK)
        Picks on other children (21/59) (DLQ, SSK)
        Breaks things (23/53) (ACH, DLQ, PSY, SSK)
        [Disobeys parents (52/78)] (DLQ)
        [Won't obey school rules (34/75)] (DLQ)
        [Lies (47/74)] (DLQ)
        [Talks back to grown-ups (44/69)] (DLQ)
        [Can't be trusted (35/66)] (DLQ)

<50T (L) Steals (18/42)
        (L) Breaks things (16/49) (ACH, DLQ, PSY, SSK)

<40T (L) Can't sit still (22/66)
        (L) Picks on other children (8/47) (SSK)
        (L) Won't obey school rules (14/63) (DLQ)

---

*Scale range suggests reduced frequency of correlate.

Table 3-15 clearly suggests that HPR >59T reflects the effects of limited behavioral and attentional control. Although many correlates of HPR >59T are in common with DLQ >79T, primary correlates reflect inattentiveness, a high activity level, and impulsivity associated with an extroverted orientation characterized by limited frustration tolerance and poor social skills.

Table 3-16

Social Skills Scale (SSK): Presenting Complaints and Parental Concerns

Total Sample:
>   Has few or no friends   (.65, 57)
>   Plays alone most of the time   (.56, .50)
>   Is picked on by other children   (.38, .34)
>   Fights with other children   (.30, .31)
>   Acts younger than real age   (.29, .32)
>   Picks on other children   (.26, .25)
>   Demands too much attention   (.23, .25)
>   Very shy   (.29, .22)
>   Is sad or unhappy much of the time   (.28, .20)
>   Is afraid to go to school   (.20, .25)
>   Says or does strange or peculiar things   (.20, .19)
>   Breaks things   (.22, .18)
>   Afraid of many things   (.27, .17)
>   Cries a lot   (.28, .17)
>   Is often confused or in a daze   (.21, .16)
>   Talks back to grown-ups   (.16, .21)
>   Clumsy or accident prone   (.16, .20)
>   Mood changes quickly or without reason   (.23, .14)
>   Disobeys parents   (.13, .21)
>   Has temper tantrums   (.25, .12)

	Child	Adolescent
Females Only:		
Slow to first walk by self	.39	.24
Refuses to go to bed	.28	.32
Males Only:		
Wants things to be perfect	.27	.21

	Male	Female
Adolescents Only:		
Fakes being sick	.20	.28
Won't obey school rules	.29	.33

Correlate Placement:
>79T [Breaks things (35/56)] (ACH, DLQ, PSY, HPR)

Table 3-16 Continued (SSK)
Correlate Placement:

> 69T Has few or no friends (23/77) (DLQ, PSY)
       Plays alone most of the time (22/68) (D, PSY, WDL)
       [Has temper tantrums (50/64)] (DLQ, PSY)
       [Fights with other children (37/63)] (DLQ, HPR)
       [Is afraid to go to school (10/26)] (D, WDL, ANX)

> 59T Demands too much attention (41/63) (ANX)
       [Is picked on by other children (27/59)] (ANX, PSY)
       [Picks on other children (27/50)] (DLQ, HPR)

< 50T (L)* Is picked on by other children (15/52)
       (L)   Fights with other children (17/53)
       (L)   Has few or no friends (4/55) (D, PSY)
       (L)   Plays alone most of the time (6/49) (WDL, PSY)
       (L)   [Picks on other children (15/45)] (HPR)
       (L)   [Breaks things (15/43)] (ACH, DLQ, PSY, HPR)

---

*Scale range suggests reduced frequency of correlate.

SSK in excess of 69T suggests frequent parental concern over the limited social interactions and skills of the child described. This analysis suggests that the reason for these limited friendships would best be sought by evaluation of other PIC scale elevations (e.g., DLQ, HPR, D, ANX, WDL).

CHAPTER 4

School Behavior and Teacher Ratings

This chapter presents the relationship between PIC profile scale variation and teacher ratings and school performance. Where robust relationships are documented, these data allow the PIC to predict diagnostically invaluable material often obtainable only at a considerable cost of both manpower and delay in scheduling or completion of an evaluation. The areas in which significant relationships are not found represent, we feel, those dimensions where teacher observation is either not relevant or is not consistently viewed by school personnel as crucial to the functioning of the educational enterprise. This interpretation, rather than one which supports the poor performance of various PIC profile scales, was selected because the majority of the scales that have few or no robust school correlates have a substantial number from parents and psychiatric residents. In addition, when robust school correlates are obtained, the dimensions described are very relevant to the school experience (e.g., ACH, HPR).

The impact of school ratings on the evaluation of PIC scale performance is great, due to the fact that these ratings are obtained from a source totally independent of the descriptions of child behavior presented on this Inventory. Indeed, these analyses suggest that parents can relay, at a molecular level, via individual Inventory responses, accurate and useful diagnostic information about school performance and cognitive abilities. This information appears, in addition, to have been enhanced by the scale construction process in transformation of molecular observations into estimates of complex academically relevant dimensions, such as behavioral hyperactivity and developmental delay.

The scales are presented below in the order in which they appear on the PIC profile. Comments are often omitted for limited or absent correlate results.

Table 4-1

Lie Scale (L): School Behavior and Teacher Ratings

Adolescents Only:	Male	Female
Poor class attendance	-.20	-.22
Children Only:		
Recommend transfer to vocational		
training program	.22	.28

Table 4-2

F Scale (F): School Behavior and Teacher Ratings

Females Only:	Child	Adolescent
Doesn't obey until threatened with		
punishment	.33	.27
Has no friends	.34	.40
Reacts with defiance to instructions		
or commands	.50	.27
Adolescents Only:		
Recommend transfer to special education		
class: Emotionally impaired	.24	.32

Table 4-3

Adjustment Scale (ADJ): School Behavior and Teacher Ratings

Total Sample:
Openly strikes back with angry behavior to teasing of other children (.26, .22)
Displays physical aggression toward objects or persons   (.24, .22)
Teacher rating of magnitude of problem   (.20, .32)
Distorts truth by making statements contrary to fact   (.19, .21)
Reacts with defiance to instructions or commands   (.20, .18)
Doesn't obey until threatened with punishment   (.17, .21)
Has difficulty concentrating for any length of time   (.14, .21)
Habitually rejects school experience through actions or comments (.14, .13)
Doesn't conform to limits on his/her own without control from others (.12, .31)
Poor study skills   (.12, .12)

Males Only:	Child	Adolescent
Disturbs other children: teasing, provoking		
fights, interrupting others	.21	.23

Table 4 -3 Continued (ADJ)
Females Only:

Easily distracted by ordinary classroom stimuli	.32	.31
Doesn't pay attention in class	.29	.30
Frequent daydreaming	.41	.28
Distractible/limited concentration	.31	.27

Adolescents Only:

Doesn't complete homework	.20	.24
Doesn't complete class assignments	.25	.35
Bored/not interested	.21	.30
Recommend transfer to special education class: Emotionally impaired	.35	.34

Correlate Placement:

>99T Doesn't conform to limits on his/her own without control from others (59/76)
   Displays physical aggression toward objects or persons (39/56)
   Reacts with defiance to instructions or commands (35/70)

>89T Openly strikes back with angry behavior to teasing of other children (32/55)
   Habitually rejects the school experience through actions or comments (35/47)

>79T Teacher rating of magnitude of problem (62/84)
   Distorts the truth by making statements contrary to fact (33/54)
   Doesn't obey until threatened with punishment (30/49)

<60T (L)* Doesn't obey until threatened with punishment (30/49)

---

*Scale range suggests reduced frequency of correlate.

ADJ reflects poor school performance and poor adjustment to the school environment. Although interpretive guidelines emphasize inability or unwillingness to comply with the rules and structure of school, the general correlate analysis lends support for the accuracy of the school rating data by highlighting the age and sex differences that are often related to poor school performance. This analysis suggests that the complaint of poor school adjustment, when evaluated at a guidance facility, is often associated with dyscontrol for males, cognitive limitations for females, and limited motivation for adolescents. It seems reasonable to expect that children with clear cognitive limitations or chronic disruptive behavior would be identified by the school and receive special attention prior to adolescence. The sex differences obtained may reflect actual sex differences in rates of symptoms (e.g., disruptive behavior) as well as a systematic bias to refer males more quickly for psychometric evaluation and special placement, perhaps because disruptive behavior is more likely to accompany cognitive limitations for boys.

Table 4-4

Achievement Scale (ACH): School Behavior and Teacher Ratings

Total Sample:
   Below average achievement in:
      Mathematics   (.33, .31)
      Reading comprehension   (.40, .30)
      Phonic skills   (.36, .30)
      Spelling   (.37, .29)
      Verbal expression   (.35, .28)
      English/language skills   (.33, .24)
      Handwriting   (.33, .23)
   Gives up easily/expects failure   (.24, .24)
   Below average intelligence   (.29, .23)
   Has difficulty understanding instructions   (.23, .26)
   Has difficulty concentrating for any length of time   (.26, .21)
   Teacher rating of magnitude of problem   (.21, .20)
   Doesn't pay attention in class   (.31, .19)
   Approaches new tasks and situations with an "I can't do it" response
      (.22, .19)
   Doesn't complete class assignments   (.22, .17)
   Recommend transfer to special education class: Emotionally impaired
      (.24, .16)
   Frequent daydreaming   (.25, .14)
   Speech problems (articulation/phonation)   (.14, .23)
   Doesn't conform to limits on his/her own without control from others
      (.13, .20)

Adolescents Only:	**Male**	**Female**
Lacks basic skills from previous classes	.46	.29
Doesn't complete tasks attempted	.33	.29
Poor study skills	.27	.25
Openly strikes back with angry behavior	.22	.31
Bored/not interested	.20	.24

Females Only:	**Child**	**Adolescent**
Recommend transfer to special education class:		
Mentally impaired (mentally retarded)	.43	.24
Child has repeated a grade	.26	.24

Correlate Placement:
>79T Frequent daydreaming (26/40)
      Approaches new tasks and situations with an "I can't do it" response
         (33/63) (DVL)
      Gives up easily/expects failure (23/49) (IS, DVL)
      [Has difficulty understanding instructions (18/35)] (DVL)
      [Below average intelligence (7/33)] (IS, DVL)
      [Transfer to special education: Emotionally impaired (8/27)] (DVL)
      [Speech problems (articulation/phonation) (6/16)] (DVL)

Table 4-4 Continued (ACH)
Correlate Placement:

> 69T   Below average achievement in: Handwriting (29/65) (DVL)
>   Below average achievement in: Verbal expression (23/54) (IS, DVL)
>   [Teacher rating of magnitude of problem (71/83)] (DVL, HPR)
>   [Doesn't pay attention in class (32/57)] (DVL, (HPR)
>   Child has repeated a grade (8/24) [Females only]

> 59T   Has difficulty concentrating for any length of time (59/76)
>   Below average achievement in: Reading comprehension (31/73) (IS, DVL)
>   Below average achievement in: Mathematics (39/73 (IS, DVL)
>   Below average achievement in: English/language skills (36/72) (IS, DVL)
>   Below average achievement in: Spelling (30/70) (IS, DVL)
>   Below average achievement in: Phonic skills (26/69) (IS, DVL)
>   Doesn't complete class assignments (34/55) (DVL)
>   [Below average achievement in: Physical education (7/46)] (IS, DVL)
>   [Children only]

< 50T (L)* Below average achievement in: Verbal expression (10/37) (DVL)
     (L)   Below average achievement in: Handwriting (11/45) (DVL)
     (L)   Below average achievement in: Reading comprehension (13/63)
            (DVL)

---

*Scale range suggests reduced frequency of correlate.

ACH interpretation appears, from Table 4-4, to clearly change with increasing scale elevation. Correlates of scores limited to 60-69T reflect poor school performance in all basic areas of achievement. Increasing elevations reflect the additional suggestion of poor performance in more basic skill areas (handwriting, verbal expression). High levels of ACH are likely to be related to both pronounced and chronic retarded achievement. ACH>79T correlates reflect the presence of a negative self-concept related to academic performance and associated withdrawal from academic activities.

Table 4-5

Intellectual Screening Scale (IS): School Behavior and Teacher Ratings

---

Total Sample:
   Below average achievement in:
      Reading comprehension   (.32, .35)
      Spelling   (.31, .34)
      Phonic skills   (.29, .33)
      Mathematics   (.27, .37)
      Handwriting   (.26, .34)
      English/language skills   (.25, .31)
      Verbal expression   (.24, .30)

Table 4-5 Continued (IS)
Total Sample:
Repeats one idea, thought, or activity over and over   (.32, .30)
Other children act as if he/she were taboo or tainted   (.24, .24)
Lacks basic skills from previous classes   (.20, .23)
Has problems with vision   (.19, .17)
Below average intelligence   (.27, .16)
Recommend transfer to special education class:
   Mentally impaired (Mentally retarded)   (.21, .16)
   Learning disabled   (.13, .20)
Has emotional problems   (.18, .15)

Adolescents Only:	**Male**	**Female**
Has enuresis (wets bed)	.28	.32
Utters nonsense syllables and/or babbles to self	.23	.31

Children Only:		
Below average achievement in: Physical education	.27	.43

Females Only:	**Child**	**Adolescent**
Has difficulty understanding instructions	.32	.25

Correlate Placement:
>89T Other children act as if he/she were taboo or tainted (17/54) (SSK)
   Repeats one idea, thought, or activity over and over (15/50) (PSY)
   Has problems with vision (12/28)
   Below average intelligence (7/34) (ACH, DVL)
   [Gives up easily/expects failure (24/44)] (ACH, DVL)
   [Transfer to special education: Learning disabled (8/22)] (DVL)
   [Tranfer to special education: Mentally impaired (Mentally retarded) (1/12)] (DVL)

>79T Below average achievement in: Verbal expression (27/56)] (ACH, DVL)
   Utters nonsense syllables and/or babbles to self (8/28) [Adolescents only]
   Below average achievement in: Physical education (18/64) (ACH, DVL) [Children only]

>69T Below average achievement in: Handwriting (29/62) (ACH, DVL)
   Lacks basic skills from previous classes (17/39) (DVL)
   Has enuresis (wets bed) (1/12) [Adolescents only]

>59T [Below average achievement in: Reading comprehension (34/74)] (ACH, DVL)
   [Below average achievement in: Mathematics (41/73)] (ACH, DVL)
   [Below average achievement in: English/language skills (39/72)] (ACH, DVL)
   [Below average achievement in: Spelling (37/66)] (ACH, DVL)
   [Below average achievement in: Phonic skills (32/66)] (ACH, DVL)

IS correlates reflect the effects of some limitation in cognitive abilities for elevations 70-89T. IS scores >89T identify children who are classified as intellectually limited by both teachers and peers. Peers are likely to reject these children, and their teachers question the need for special education services.

Table 4-6

Development Scale (DVL): School Behavior and Teacher Ratings

Total Sample:
  Below average achievement in:
    Reading comprehension   (.37, .30)
    Mathematics   (.33, .30)
    Phonic skills   (.34, .28)
    Spelling   (.34, .27)
    Verbal expression (.34, .26)
    English/language skills   (.30, .25)
    Handwriting   (..32, .23)
    Physical education   (.23, .22)
  Difficulty understanding instructions   (.26, .28)
  Lacks basic skills from previous classes   (.22, .24)
  Below average intelligence   (.27, .22)
  Approaches new tasks with an "I can't do it" response   (..22, .23)
  Gives up easily/expects failure   (.21, .22)
  Teacher rating of magnitude of problem   (.19, .24)
  Recommend transfer to special education class:
    Emotionally impaired   (.20, .19)
    Mentally impaired (Mentally retarded)   (.18, .25)
    Learning disabled   (.22, .16)
  Doesn't pay attention in class   (.29, .18)
  Doesn't complete tasks attempted   (.21, .22)
  Easily distracted by ordinary classroom stimuli   (.18, .21)
  Poor study skills   (.16, .15)
  Doesn't complete class assignments   (.22, .15)
  Speech problems (articulation/phonation)   (.13, .23)

	Child	Adolescent
Males Only:		
Has difficulty concentrating for any length of time	.21	.28

	Male	Female
Adolescents Only:		
Distractible/limited concentration	.21	.23

Correlate Placement:
> 79T   Transfer to special education: Emotionally impaired (11/30) (ACH)
    Transfer to special education: Learning disabled (7/26) (IS)
    Speech problems (articulation/phonation) (6/19) (ACH)
    Transfer to special education: Mentally impaired (mentally retarded) (1/14) (IS)
    [Gives up easily/expects failure (24/49)] (ACH, IS)
    [Below average intelligence (8/33)] (ACH, IS)

Table 4-6 Continued (DVL)
Correlate Placement:

> 69T Below average achievement in: Physical education (17/43) (ACH, IS)
        Has difficulty understanding instructions (14/43) (ACH)
        [Teacher rating of magnitude of problem (72/83)] (ACH, HPR)
        [Below average achievement in: Handwriting (31/69)] (ACH, IS)
        [Below average achievement in: Verbal expression (23/62)] (ACH, IS)
        [Approaches new tasks and situations with "I can't do it" response (31/51)]
          (ACH)
        Poor fine motor coordination (drawing, etc.) (15/31) [Male children only]

> 59T Easily distracted away from tasks at hand by ordinary classroom stimuli
          (57/70)
        Poor study skills (27/42)
        Doesn't complete tasks attempted (56/71) (DLQ)
        [Below average achievement in: Mathematics (41/75)] (ACH, IS)
        [Below average achievement in: Spelling (33/72)] (ACH, IS)
        [Below average achievement in: Reading comprehension (38/72)] (ACH,
          IS)
        [Below average achievement in: Phonic skills (31/70)] (ACH, IS)
        [Below average achievement in: English/language skills (43/70)] (ACH,
          IS)
        [Doesn't complete class assignments (38/54)] (ACH)
        [Doesn't pay attention in class (30/50)] (ACH)
        [Lacks basic skills from previous classes (13/35)] (IS)

< 50T (L)* Has difficulty understanding instructions (5/24)
        (L) Below average achievement in: Physical education (6/28)
        (L) Lacks basic skills from previous classes (9/28)
        (L) Gives up easily/expects failure (14/30)
        (L) Below average achievement in: Phonic skills (18/59)
        (L) Below average achievement in: Spelling (19/62)
        (L) [Below average achievement in: Verbal expression (5/40)] (ACH)
        (L) [Below average achievement in: Handwriting (15/46)] (ACH)
        (L) [Below average achievement in: Reading comprehension (16/63)]
          (ACH)

---

*Scale range suggests reduced frequency of correlate.

DVL correlates, like the descriptors of ACH and IS, reflect poor academic performance. In addition, DVL suggests behaviors that reflect the developmental delay previously documented by parents: poor fine and gross motor coordination and problems in speech development. DVL >79T suggests that the child's teacher is concerned that a special class placement may be necessary to insure optimal academic growth.

Table 4-7

Depression Scale (D): School Behavior and Teacher Ratings

Females Only:	Child	Adolescent
Doesn't engage in group activities	.39	.27
Has few or no friends	.31	.32

Correlate Placement:

>89T [Is hypercritical of self (10/57)] (ANX) [Female adolescents only]
   [Refers to self as dumb, stupid, or incapable (13/36)] (ANX) [Female
   adolescents only]

>79T Expresses concern about being lonely, unhappy (21/47)] (ANX) [Female
   adolescents only]

D obtained results in these analyses limited only to females, perhaps reflecting the fact that females are more open to the expression of such feelings and concerns. However, teachers are also less likely to probe for such content in compliant students, and interactions suggesting depression are less likely to occur under the teacher's observation.

Table 4-8

Delinquency Scale (DLQ): School Behavior and Teacher Ratings

Total Sample:

   Habitually rejects the school experience through actions or comments
   (.26, .27)

   Reacts with defiance to instructions or commands   (.30, .23)

   Doesn't conform to limits on his/her own without control from others
   (.23, .28)

   Poor class attendance   (.24, .22)

   Steals things from other children   (.23, .22)

   Doesn't obey until threatened with punishment   (.22, .20)

   Bored/not interested   (.19, .30)

   Distorts the truth by making statements contrary to fact   (.19, .29)

   Argues and must have the last word in verbal exchanges   (.15, .23)

   Complains about others' unfairness and/or discrimination toward him/her
   (.14, .27)

   Doesn't complete tasks attempted   (.14, .27)

   Displays physical aggression toward objects or persons   (.13, .24)

   Openly strikes back with angry behavior to teasing of other children
   (.13, .21)

   Recommend transfer to special education class: Emotionally impaired
   (.12, .19)

Table 4-8 Continued (DLQ)

Adolescents Only:	Male	Female
Has difficulty concentrating for any length of time	.25	.40
Easily distracted away from task at hand by ordinary classroom stimuli	.27	.43
Doesn't complete homework	.19	.31

Children Only:		
Has temper tantrums	.22	.31

Males Only:	Child	Adolescent
Disturbs other children: teasing, provoking fights, interrupting others	.26	.27

Correlate Placement:

>109T Poor class attendance (20/48)

> 99T Bored/not interested (24/49)

> 89T Habitually rejects the school experience through actions or comments (33/55)
Reacts with defiance to instructions or commands (31/51) (HPR)
[Transfer to special education: Emotionally impaired (9/19)] (ACH, DVL)

>79T Complains about others' unfairness and/or discrimination toward him/her (39/59) (HPR)
Distorts the truth by making statements contrary to fact (34/58) (HPR)
Doesn't obey until threatened with punishment (32/50) (HPR)
Argues and must have the last word in verbal exchanges (28/46) (HPR)
[Displays physical aggression toward objects or persons (32/52)] (HPR)
[Openly strikes back with angry behavior to teasing of other children (31/51)] (HPR, SSK)
[Steals things from other children (5/21)] (HPR)

> 59T [Doesn't complete tasks attempted (33/68)] (DVL)
[Doesn't conform to limits on his/her own without control from others (29/67)] (HPR)

< 60T (L)* Poor class attendance (4/27)
(L)   Habitually rejects the school experience through actions or comments (16/43)
(L)   Reacts with defiance to instructions or commands (11/42) (HPR)
(L)   Argues and must have the last word in verbal exchanges (16/40) (HPR)
(L)   [Displays physical aggression toward objects or persons (16/46)] (HPR)

---

*Scale range suggests reduced frequency of correlate.

DLQ elevation clearly reflects an inability to comply with the structure and limits of school, as it does in the home environment. DLQ reflects poorly modulated hostility as manifest by provocation, argumentativeness, and projection of blame. DLQ >79T is associated with teacher observation of fighting, lying, or stealing at school. DLQ elevation is associated with a teacher's concern that the behavior displayed will require placement in a special education classroom for the emotionally impaired.

Table 4-9

Withdrawal Scale (WDL): School Performance and Teacher Ratings

	Child	Adolescent
Total Sample:		
Is overactive, restless, and/or continually shifting body positions (.21, .29)		
Doesn't engage in group activities (.28, .16)		
Females Only:		
Approaches new tasks and situations with an "I can't do it" response	.31	.25
Adolescents Only:		
Has few or no friends	.22	.39
Correlate Placement:		
>69T Doesn't engage in group activities (31/51)		

WDL reflects teacher observations of social isolation as it relates to similar parental observations.

Table 4-10

Anxiety Scale (ANX): School Performance and Teacher Ratings

Correlate Placement:

>89T Refers to self as dumb, stupid, or incapable (15/67) (D)
[Female adolescents only]

>79T Is hypercritical of self (13/50) (D) [Female adolescents only]

>69T [Expresses concern about being lonely, unhappy (21/45)] (D)
[Female adolescents only]

The same school correlates selected for D were obtained for ANX.

Table 4-11

Psychosis Scale (PSY): School Performance and Teacher Ratings

---

Total Sample:
    Repeats one idea, thought, or activity over and over   (.24, .22)
    Has few or no friends   (.23, .14)

Females Only:	**Child**	**Adolescent**
Becomes hysterical, upset, or angry when		
things don't go his way	.33	.29
Has temper tantrums	.41	.26
Children Only:	**Male**	**Female**
Shuns or avoids heterosexual activities	.21	.39

Correlate Placement:

>99T Shuns or avoids heterosexual activities (5/36) [Children only]

>89T [Has few or no friends (24/41)] (SSK)
    [Repeats one idea, thought, or activity over and over (14/34)] (IS)

>79T Becomes hysterical, upset, or angry when things do not go his way
    (19/55) [Females only]

<50T (L)* [Has few or no friends (8/30)] (SSK)

---

*Scale range suggests reduced frequency of correlate.

PSY correlates, although few in this nonpsychotic sample, reflect limited interpersonal skills, preoccupation, and social isolation.

Table 4-12

Hyperactivity Scale (HPR): School Performance and Teacher Ratings

---

Total Sample:
    Disturbs other children: teasing, provoking fights, interrupting others
    (.54, .35)
    Impulsively reacts (behaves) without thinking   (.37, .35)
    Talkative   (.35, .36)
    Is overactive, restless, and/or continually shifting body
    positions   (.33, .40)
    Continually seeks attention   (.46, .30)
    Openly strikes back with angry behavior to teasing of other children
    (.42, .30)
    Doesn't conform to limits on his/her own without control from others
    (.30, .34)
    Displays physical aggression toward objects or persons   (.46, .29)
    Distorts the truth by making statements contrary to fact   (.41, .29)

Table 4-12 Continued (HPR)
Total Sample:

Doesn't obey until threatened with punishment   (.35, .29)
Restless/fidgety   (.27, .28)
Teacher rating of magnitude of problem   (.25, .33)
Argues and must have the last word in verbal exchanges   (.47, .24)
Reacts with defiance to instructions or commands   (.37, .23)
Doesn't pay attention in class   (.28, .23)
Steals things from other children   (.25, .23)
Complains about others' unfairness and/or discrimination toward him/her
   (.22, .24)
When teased or irritated by other children, takes out his/her frustration(s)
   on another inappropriate person or thing   (.31, .22)
Makes distrustful or suspicious remarks about actions of others toward
   him/her   (.21, .22)
Tries to avoid calling attention to self   (-.19, -.25)
Has temper tantrums   (.26, .19)
Poor study skills   (.18, .18)
Doesn't complete homework   (.14, .17)
Doesn't engage in group activities   (-.30, -.14)

Adolescents Only:	Male	Female
Recommend transfer to special education class: Emotionally impaired	.29	.24
Recommend transfer to vocational training program	.19	.23

Correlate Placement:

>79T Recommend transfer to vocational training program (3/15)
     [Adolescents only]

>69T Has temper tantrums (25/45)
     Doesn't complete homework (24/38)
     (L)* Doesn't engage in group activities (42/26)
     Displays physical aggression toward objects or persons (31/67)
     Openly strikes back with angry behavior to teasing of other children
        (39/63) (DLQ, SSK)
     Steals things from other children (8/24) (DLQ)
     [Distorts the truth by making statements contrary to fact (36/67)] (DLQ)
     [Complains about others' unfairness and/or discrimination toward him
        (43/62)] (DLQ)
     [Reacts with defiance to instructions or commands (31/54)] (DLQ)

>59T Disturbs other children: teasing, provoking fights, interrupting others
        (28/73)
     Is overactive, restless, and/or continually shifting body positions (29/64)
     Continually seeks attention (25/62)
     Impulsively reacts (behaves) without thinking (22/56)
     Makes distrustful or suspicious remarks about actions of others toward
        him (27/48)
     Talkative (16/47)

Table 4-12 Continued 59T (HPR)
Correlate Placement:

When teased or irritated by other children, takes out his/ her frustration(s) on another inappropriate person or thing (18/45)

Restless/fidgety (18/44)

(L) Tries to avoid calling attention to self (33/16)

Doesn't conform to limits on his/her own without control from others (45/76) (DLQ)

Doesn't pay attention in class (27/51) (ACH, DVL)

[Teacher rating of magnitude of problem (64/83)] (ACH, DVL)

[Doesn't obey until threatened with punishment (29/51)] (ACH, DVL)

[Poor study skills (25/43)] (DVL)

[Argues and must hive the last word in verbal exchanges (19/35)] (DVL)

< 50T (L) When teased or irritated by other children, takes out his/ her frustration(s) on another inappropriate person or thing (14/40)

(L) Continually seeks attention (22/54)

(L) [Argues and must have the last word in verbal exchanges (13/45)] (DLQ)

< 40T (L) Talkative (4/37)

(L) Disturbs other children: teasing, provoking fights, interrupting others (11/58)

(L) Impulsively reacts (behaves) without thinking (12/45)

(L) Restless/fidgety (14/35)

(L) Doesn't obey until threatened with punishment (14/45)

(L) Openly strikes back with angry behavior to teasing of other children (14/45 (SSK)

(L) [Displays physical aggression toward objects or persons (14/46)] (DLQ)

(L) [Reacts with defiance to instructions or commands (14/41)] (DLQ)

---

*Scale range suggests reduced frequency of correlate.

The substantial number of unique and primary HPR correlates reflects the importance of this scale in reflecting disrupted school adjustment. HPR > 59T suggests overactivity, impulsivity, restlessness, and distractibility coupled with a high level of sociability. Higher HPR elevations (>69T) suggest, *in addition*, a superimposed adjustment characterized by limited frustration tolerance, undercontrolled hostility, and manipulative/antisocial behavior. It is interesting to note that the only correlate of HPR > 79T is "Transfer to vocational training program" for adolescents. Perhaps this reflects the most reasonable educational placement for those children who progressed through school with an essentially uncontrolled hyperactivity syndrome.

Table 4-13

Social Skills Scale (SSK): School Performance and Teacher Ratings

Total Sample:
    Has no friends   (.28, .20)
    Repeats one idea, thought, or activity over and over   (.17, .24)
    Other children act as if he/she were taboo or tainted   (.25, .16)
    Openly strikes back with angry behavior to teasing of other children
        (.24, .15)
    Doesn't initiate relationships with other children   (.19, .14)

Females Only:	**Child**	**Adolescent**
Reacts with defiance to instructions or commands	.39	.34

Adolescents Only:	**Male**	**Female**
Recommend transfer to special education class: Emotionally impaired	.28	.25

Correlate Placement:
>79T Has no friends (23/44) (PSY)
    [Openly strikes back with angry behavior to teasing of other children
        (38/54)] (DLQ, HPR)
    [Other children act as if he/she were taboo or tainted (21/38)] (IS)

>69T Doesn't initiate relationships with other children (26/42)

<50T (L)* Other children act as if he/she were taboo or tainted (0/27)
    (L)   Has no friends (9/30) (PSY)
    (L)   [Openly strikes back with angry behavior to teasing of other children
        (16/44)] (HPR)

*Scale range suggests reduced frequency of correlate.

SSK >69T clearly reflects an inability to make and keep friends in both the home neighborhood and at school. The reduction in the clarity of the relationship between SSK and social activity in the classroom versus at home is likely to reflect errors of omission in teacher ratings. This explanation is supported by the fact that the identical correlate "Has [few or] no friends" was optimally placed at >69T for parent informant and at >79T for teacher informant. This correlate is accurate for 77% of parent ratings and only 44% of teacher ratings.

CHAPTER 5

Clinical Descriptors and Ratings

This chapter summarizes the PIC scale correlates from the diagnostic evaluation usually completed by a psychiatric resident in his second to fourth year of training. In effect, correlates from these analyses predict the impressions and disposition likely to be achieved by a psychiatric evaluation.

The psychiatric evaluation compiles information from diverse sources. Statements offered by the primary informants, parents/guardians, regarding behavior problems were available to the clinician prior to the interview. Observations and recommendations from school personnel were also typically available, as well as supporting documents, such as previous psychological testing, social work contacts, etc. These checklists provided independent descriptors of the child's behavior in relatively diverse settings. In addition to supplying an initial impression of the child, these data also helped structure the interview by suggesting problem areas in need of further investigation. The clinical evaluation itself involved reviewing the available data, interviewing the child and his parent/guardian, and completing a physical and neurological examination. As described previously, the clinician rating form covered a variety of content domains relevant to child and adolescent psychopathology: affect, cognitive/neurological functioning, interpersonal relations, physical development and health, family relations, parent description, and ideal recommendations. Not only did the checklist provide for a behavioral description of the problem child, it also required specific psychiatric judgments unavailable from other sources, e.g., "displays an associative (thought) disorder," "displays receptive aphasic symptoms." The completed checklist represents a synthesis of these various data sources.

The scales are again presented in the order in which they appear in the PIC profile. Comments are omitted for limited or absent correlate results.

Table 5-1

Lie Scale (L): Clinical Descriptors and Ratings

Total Sample:

Disobedient to parents   (-.33, -.28)

Lying   (-.34, -.24)

Running away from home   (-.21, -.18)

Usually expects failure   (-.18, -.18)

Poor judgment/needs much supervision   (-.16, -.25)

Complains of poor concentration/is easily distracted   (-.16, -.19)

Described as being selfish   (-.24, -.12)

Males Only:	**Child**	**Adolescent**
Destructive of objects	-.27	-.26
Impulsive behavior	-.24	-.22

Adolescents Only:	**Male**	**Female**
Often a poor sport and poor loser	-.25	-.23
Involved with the police	-.23	-.25

Children Only:		
Overly controlling/bossy	-.23	-.30

Correlate Placement:

>59T (L)* Poor judgment/needs much supervision (55/25) (ADJ)

　　　(L)   Running away from home (28/8)

>49T (L)   Disobedient to parents (69/35) (ADJ)

　　　(L)   Complains of poor concentration/is easily distracted (57/35)

　　　(L)   Lying (54/26) (ADJ)

---

*Scale range suggests reduced frequency of correlate.

Correlates for the L scale were all inversely related to scale elevation. Minimal elevations suggest that impulsive, aggressive behaviors are less likely to occur.

Table 5-2

F Scale (F): Clinical Descriptors and Ratings

Total Sample:

Poor prognosis for remediation of current problems   (.26, .24)

Refer for psychiatric hospitalization   (.21, .21)

Mother overly permissive, difficulty in setting limits   (.19, .19)

Displays irresponsible behavior   (.16, .27)

Destructive of objects   (.18, .16)

Temper tantrums   (.12, .25)

Table 5-2 Continued (F)

Females Only:	Child	Adolescent
Disobedience to teachers or breaks school rules	.33	.25

Children Only:	Male	Female
Awakens early	.27	.37

Correlate Placement:

$>$109T Destructive of objects (35/58) (ADJ)

$>$ 99T Displays irresponsible behavior (44/59)
Refer for psychiatric hospitalization (31/47)

$>$ 89T Mother overly permissive, difficulty in setting limits (35/57)
Temper tantrums (39/55) (ADJ)

Replicated correlates for the F scale suggest overt, aggressive behavior difficulties. Referral for inpatient care indicates the relatively severe nature of symptoms reflected by elevations $>$ 99T.

Table 5-3

Adjustment Scale (ADJ): Clinical Descriptors and Ratings

Total Sample:

Disobedient to parents   (.25, .31)
Temper tantrums   (.24, .27)
Lying   (.23, .31)
Described as being selfish   (.21, .30)
Destructive of objects   (.20, .29)
Expects rejection from others   (.20, .25)
Overactive or agitated   (.20, .24)
Disobedience to teachers or breaks school rules   (.19, .25)
Mother inconsistent in setting limits   (.19, .28)
Poor judgment/needs much supervision   (.19, .23)
Often a poor sport and poor loser   (.19, .16)
Usually expects failure   (.24, .18)
Stealing   (.14, .27)

Males Only:	Child	Adolescent
Impulsive behavior	.40	.36
Previous psychotropic medication: Stimulants	.40	.29
Mother is emotionally disturbed (in need of individual treatment)	.23	.25

Children Only:	Male	Female
Isolative (usually plays alone, stays in room, etc.)	.21	.37

Table 5-3 Continued (ADJ)

Adolescents Only:	Male	Female
Involved with the police	.28	.25
Poor prognosis for remediation of current problems	.24	.25

Correlate Placement:

>109T Overly critical of self (23/38)

> 99T Lying (43/67) (L)
       Disobedience to teachers or breaks school rules (45/66)
       Stealing (28/47)

> 89T Disobedient to parents (53/75) (L)
       Poor judgment/needs much supervision (46/63) (L)
       Temper tantrums (33/58) (F)
       Destructive of objects (29/51) (F)
       Described as being selfish (16/36)

ADJ correlates describe a variety of behaviors of an externalizing, acting-out nature. Hostility, dyscontrol, and difficulties accepting limits are accurately reflected in ADJ scale elevations >89T. The disruptive quality of these behaviors frequently motivates parents to seek professional intervention.

Table 5-4

Achievement Scale (ACH): Clinical Descriptors and Ratings

Total Sample:

Achievement in school at least one year below chronological age grade placement (underachievement)   (.47, .41)

Functions at below average intellectual level   (.45, .39)

Displays expressive aphasic symptoms (unable to find word to express ideas; uses general or related words rather than specific word desired)   (.28, .25)

Speech disturbance:

    Immature   (.22, .32)

    Phonation   (.27, .21)

    Articulation   (.20, .20)

Poor judgment/needs much supervision   (.22, .29)

Concrete thinking beyond age expectation   (.21, .34)

Gross motor ataxia (clumsiness): Mild   (.21, .26)

Mute/primitive verbal skills   (.28, .20)

Poor prognosis for remediation of current problems   (.20, .23)

Untidy and careless in self-appearance   (.19, .21)

Previous psychotropic medication: Stimulants (.30, .17)

Specific recommendations given to school   (.17, .24)

Table 5-4 Continued (ACH)
Total Sample:
 Impulsive behavior   (.17, .22)
 Decreased verbal communication/seldom talks   (.16, .25)
 Fine motor ataxia (clumsiness): Mild   (.15, .32)
 Destructive of objects   (.14, .22)
 Displays receptive aphasic symptoms (doesn't seem to comprehend spoken
  language well)   (.11, .24)

Children Only: **Male** **Female**
 Recommend major tranquilizers for child   .19   .30

Correlate Placement:
>79T Mute/primitive verbal skills (11/29)
  [Poor prognosis for remediation of current problems (48/76)] (DVL, DLQ)
  [Poor judgment/needs much supervision (50/74)] (DVL, PSY)
  [Concrete thinking beyond age expectation (18/45)] (DVL, PSY)
  [Untidy and careless in self-appearance (9/34)] (IS, DVL)
  [Decreased verbal communication/seldom talks (18/34)] (IS, DVL)
  [Speech disturbance: Articulation (14/34)] (IS, DVL)
  [Speech disturbance: Phonation (5/26)] (DVL, PSY)
  [Displays receptive aphasic symptoms (doesn't seem to comprehend
  spoken language well) (6/20)] (IS, DVL)

>69T Achievement in school at least one year below chronological age grade
  placement (underachievement) (47/84) (IS, DVL)
  [Functions at below average intellectual level: Mild (20/40); Moderate/
  Severe (9/26)] (DVL)
  [Specific recommendations to school (25/43)] (DVL)
  [Fine motor ataxia (clumsiness): Mild (15/36)] (IS, DVL)
  [Previous psychotropic medication: Stimulants (15/33)] (IS, DVL)
  [Gross motor ataxia (clumsiness): Mild (11/27)] (IS, DVL)
  [Speech disturbance: Immature (7/25)] (IS, DVL)
  [Displays expressive aphasic symptoms (unable to find words to express
  ideas; uses general or related word rather than specific word desired
  (5/19)] (DVL)

<50T (L)* Decreased verbal communication/seldom talks (3/23)
  (L) [Concrete thinking beyond age expectation (5/24)] (DVL)

---

*Scale range suggests reduced frequency of correlate.

Examination of Table 5-4 indicates that ACH correlates suggest academic retardation as well as a variety of reasons for this underachievement: limited intellectual ability, neurological symptoms, and impulsive behavior. Further examination of the table suggests that elevations >69T reflect those poor cognitive skills likely to result in retarded academic achievement.

Table 5-5

Intellectual Screening Scale (IS): Clinical Descriptors and Ratings

Total Sample:
   Functions at below average intellectual level   (.44, .42)
   Achievement in school at least one year below chronological age grade
      placement (underachievement)   (.35, .34)
   Friends are mainly younger than child   (.28, .25)
   Speech disturbance:
      Articulation   (.27, .24)
      Immature   (.31, .24)
      Echolalia   (.30, .19)
      Phonation   (.34, .13)
   Displays receptive aphasic symptoms (doesn't seem to comprehend spoken
      language well)   (.27, .22)
   Fine motor ataxia (clumsiness): Mild   (.19, .35)
   Previous psychotropic medication: Stimulants   (.26, .16)
   Recommendation for chemotherapy represents a change from current
      chemotherapy   (.16, .20)
   Gross motor ataxia (clumsiness): Mild   (.15, .24)
   Gross motor ataxia (clumsiness): Moderate/Severe   (.33, .14)
   Isolative (usually plays alone, stays in room, etc.)   (.14, .18)
   Decreased verbal communication/seldom talks   (.13, .15)
   Displays an associative (thought) disorder   (.23, .13)
   Untidy and careless in self-appearance   (.12, .15)

	Child	Adolescent
Females Only:		
Frequent fights with siblings	.53	.25
Males Only:		
Fine motor ataxia (clumsiness): Moderate/		
Severe	.28	.24

	Male	Female
Adolescents Only:		
Nocturnal enuresis: Continuing	.23	.23
Children Only:		
Previous psychotropic medication:		
Major tranquilizers	.26	.33

Correlate Placement:
>109T Gross motor ataxia (clumsiness): Moderate/Severe (2/19)
      [Speech disturbance: Echolalia (1/18)] (PSY)

 >89T Friends are mainly younger than child (11/38)
      Functions at below average intellectual level: Moderate/Severe (11/42)
      (ACH)
      Untidy and careless in self-appearance (10/27) (ACH, DVL)
      [Speech disturbance: Articulation (13/49)] (ACH, DVL)
      [Speech disturbance: Immature (11/35)] (ACH, DVL)
      Previous psychotropic medication: Major tranquilizers (4/22)
         [Children only]

Table 5-5 Continued (IS)
Correlate Placement:
>79T [Gross motor ataxia (clumsiness): Mild (13/39)] (ACH, DVL)
      [Previous psychotropic medication: Stimulants (17/38)] (ACH, DVL)
      [Decreased verbal communication/seldom talks (17/31)] (ACH, DVL)
      [Displays receptive aphasic symptoms (doesn't seem to comprehend
        spoken language well) (5/20)] (ACH, DVL)
      Frequent fights with siblings (21/61) [Females only]
      Nocturnal enuresis: Continuing (5/21) [Adolescents only]
>69T Functions at below average intellectual level: Mild (22/37) (ACH)
      [Achievement in school at least one year below chronological age grade
        placement (underachievement) (48/80)] (ACH, DVL)
      [Fine motor ataxia (clumsiness): Mild (14/38)] (ACH, DVL)
<50T (L)* Fine motor ataxia (clumsiness): Mild (8/28)
<40T (L)   Speech disturbance: Articulation (2/18)
     (L)   Speech disturbance: Immature (0/15)

---

*Scale range suggests reduced frequency of correlate.

Replicated IS correlates reflect limited intellectual skills, poor academic achievement, withdrawal, and neurological symptoms. Elevations >69T suggest poor cognitive skills. With increasing scale elevation, neurological symptoms are more likely, as well as significant intellectual retardation. With elevations >109T, moderate to severe neurological impairment is suggested, as well as the possibility of psychotic symptoms, e.g., echolalia. As discussed previously, our sample was limited in the number of children receiving diagnosis of psychosis. It is our expectation that other investigators may find relationships between extremely elevated IS T-scores and psychotic behaviors.

Table 5-6
Development Scale (DVL): Clinical Descriptors and Ratings

Total Sample:
      Achievement in school at least one year below chronological age grade
        placement (underachievement) (.48, .41)
      Speech disturbance:
      Immature (.42, .37)
      Phonation (.27' .24)
      Articulation (.25, .21)
      Displays expressive aphasic symptoms (unable to find words to express
        ideas; uses general or related word rather than specific word desired)
        (.25, .28)
      Concrete thinking beyond age expectation (.22, .44)
      Specific recommendations to school (.22, .25)

Table 5-6 Continued (DVL)
Total Sample:

    Poor judgment/needs much supervision   (.21, .21)
    Gross motor ataxia (clumsiness): Mild   (.21' .29)
    Fine motor ataxia (clumsiness): Mild   (.18, .33)
    Displays receptive aphasic symptoms (doesn't seem to comprehend spoken
        language well)   (.17, .37)
    Poor prognosis for remediation of current problems   (.17, .21)
    Usually expects failure   (.15, .18)
    Decreased verbal communication/seldom talks 1.15, .26)
    Previous psychotropic medication: Stimulants   (.24, .14)
    Untidy and careless in self-appearance   (.11, .19)

Children Only:	**Male**	**Female**
Destructive of objects	.22	.36
Isolative (usually plays alone, stays in room, etc.)	.24	.29
Intentional enuresis: Continuing	.22	.35

Correlate Placement:

>79T Speech disturbance: Phonation (5/29) (ACH, PSY)
      [Poor judgment/needs much supervision (50/80)] (ACH, PSY)
      Retarded physical growth (5/16) [Male children only]

>69T Concrete thinking beyond age expectation (14/44) (ACH, PSY)
      Fine motor ataxia (clumsiness): Mild (16/38) (ACH, IS)
      Speech disturbance: Immature (6/33) (ACH, IS)
      Decreased verbal communication/seldom talks (15/33) (ACH, IS)
      Previous psychotropic medication: Stimulants (17/32) (ACH, IS)
      Speech disturbance: Articulation (12/29) (ACH, IS)
      Gross motor ataxia (clumsiness): Mild (12/29) (ACH, IS)
      Displays expressive aphasic symptoms (unable to find words to express
        ideas; uses general or related word rather than specific word desired)
        (5/22) (ACH)
      Displays receptive aphasic symptoms (doesn't seem to comprehend
        spoken language well) (5/17) (ACH, IS)
      [Poor prognosis for remediation of current problems (48/62)] (ACH,
        DLQ)
      [Untidy and careless in self-appearance (10/18)] (ACH, IS)

>59T Specific recommendations to school (22/40) (ACH)
      [Achievement in school at least one year below chronological age grade
        placement (underachievement) (40/78)] (ACH, IS)

<50T (L)* Specific recommendations to school (12/36)
      (L)   Concrete thinking beyond age expectation (5/26) (ACH)

---

*Scale range suggests reduced frequency of correlate.

Table 5-6 presents the replicated correlates and suggested interpretive guidelines for DVL. Correlates reflect neurological symptoms as well as underachievement. Elevations >59T suggest the need to evaluate school placement. Neurological impairment is likely with elevations >69T.

A significant number of the same replicated correlates were obtained for ACH, IS, DVL. This overlap suggest that the interpretive significance of a given scale elevation must take into consideration the elevations on the other two scales. For example, an ACH elevation in the absence of significant IS and DVL elevations suggests that analysis of other clinical scale elevations may reveal the reasons for this underachievement.

Table 5-7

Somatic Concern Scale (SOM): Clinical Descriptors and Ratings

Total Sample:		
Chronic pain (.15, .26)		
Adolescents Only:	**Male**	**Female**
Untidy and careless in self-appearance	.25	.23
Children Only:		
Child was born out of wedlock	.28	.34

Correlate Placement:
>79T   Chronic pain (3/14)
       Child was born out of wedlock (20/56) [Children only]
       Somatic response to stress (e.g., stomachaches) (16/43)
         [Male children only]
       [Separation anxiety (6/23)] (WDL) [Male children only]
> 69T   Headaches (17/42) (D) [Male adolescents only]

Table 5-8

Depression Scale (D): Clinical Descriptors and Ratings

Total Sample:		
Isolative (usually plays alone, stays in room, etc.) (.26, .33)		
Excessive shyness (.20, .24)		
Mother overly permissive, difficulty in setting limits (.20, .17)		
Has few or no friends (.24, .14)		
Overly critical of self (.28, .13)		
Children Only:	**Male**	**Female**
Frequent crying	.28	.48
Sleep disturbance: Has difficulty		
getting to sleep	.19	.37

Table 5-8 Continued (D)

Males Only:	Child	Adolescent
Expects rejection from others	.25	.22
Self-destructive behavior (wrist-slashing, head-banging, etc.)	.23	.20

Correlate Placement:

>89T Usually expects failure (31/77) [Female adolescents only]

>79T Overly critical of self (18/37) (SSK)

[Mother overly permissive, difficulty in setting limits (35/55)] (ANX)

[Excessive shyness (17/37)] (WDL, SSK)

Somatic response to stress (e.g., stomachaches) (19/55) [Male adolescents only]

Expresses suicidal thoughts or ideations (18/39) [Male adolescents only]

Worries a great deal (32/53) [Female children only]

Decreased appetite (3/32) (ANX) [Female children only]

[Headaches (20/41)] (SOM) [Male adolescents only]

>69T [Isolative (usually plays alone, stay in room, etc.) (25/52)] (WDL, PSY)

Frequent crying (21/54) [Children only]

<50T (L)* [Isolative (usually plays alone, stays in room, etc.) (15/42)] (WDL, PSY)

---

*Scale range suggests reduced frequency of correlate.

Replicated D correlates suggest social isolation and poor self-concept. Elevations >79T indicate that male adolescents are more likely to present somatizing symptomatology as well as suicidal ideation, while ruminations and eating disturbances are more likely for female children.

Table 5-9

Family Relations Scale (FAM): Clinical Descriptors and Ratings

---

Total Sample:

Parents present a history of marital discord   (.34, .42)

Mother inconsistent in setting limits   (.27, .31)

Mother emotionally disturbed (in need of individual treatment)   (.25, .35)

Father rejecting or overly critical of child   (.25, .28)

Father alcoholic or other substance abuser   (.34, .20)

Biological parents currently divorced or separated   (.27, .20)

Mother alcoholic or other substance abuser   (.23, .20)

Males Only:	Child	Adolescent
Often a poor sport and poor loser	.27	.22
Resistant to change in environment	.23	.25

Table 5-9 Continued (FAM)

Adolescents Only:	**Male**	**Female**
Father defensive (about self) in interview	.47	.41

Correlate Placement:

>79T Father rejecting or overly critical of child (28/73)
           Father uses excessive physical punishment (23/100)

>69T Parents present history of marital discord (61/91)
           Father alcoholic or other substance abuser (29/62)
           Mother alcoholic or other substance abuser (5/17)
           Mother emotionally disturbed (in need of individual treatment) (35/62)
               (DLQ)
           Father defensive (about self) in interview (31/70) [Adolescents only]
           (L)* Refer for outpatient individual therapy (29/14)
               [Female adolescents only]

>59T Biological parents are currently divorced or separated (47/68)
           Mother inconsistent in setting limits (44/69) (DLQ)
           Child expresses strong dislike of a member of the family (31/64)
               [Female adolescents only]

<50T (L) Mother emotionally disturbed (in need of individual treatment) (16/48)

---

*Scale range suggests reduced frequency of correlate.

Correlates for FAM clearly reflect family disorganization and dysfunction. Parental divorce, difficulty setting limits, and parental emotional disturbance are likely with scale elevations >59T.

Table 5-10

Delinquency Scale (DLQ): Clinical Descriptors and Ratings

Total Sample:
        Truancy   (.45, .45)
        Involved with the police   (.44, .49)
        Running away from home   (.42, .28)
        Stealing   (.31, .38)
        Disobedient to parents   (.30, .41)
        Displays irresponsible behavior   (.28, .43)
        Lying   (.26, .36)
        Mother inconsistent in setting limits   (.26, .30)
        Disobedience to teachers or breaks school rules   (.26, .30)
        Impulsive behavior   (.25, .39)
        Temper tantrums   (.27, .25)
        Verbally hostile or argumentative   (.25, .28)
        Father inconsistent in setting limits   (.27, .25)
        Friends are mainly older than child   (.30, .24)

Table 5-10 Continued (DLQ)
Total Sample:

> Refer for psychiatric hospitalization   (.33, .23)
> Poor prognosis for remediation of current problems   (.23, .28)
> Blames others for his/her problems   (.21, .22)
> Expresses a dislike for school   (.18, .38)
> Expects rejection from others   (.20, .17)
> Poor judgment/needs much supervision   (.16, .28)
> Described as being selfish   (.25, .15)
> Mother emotionally disturbed (in need of individual treatment)   (.32, .13)

Adolescents Only:	**Male**	**Female**
Unrealistic fears	-.23	-.27
Obsessive thought pattern	-.25	-.26
Compulsive or ritualistic behavior	-.21	-.23
Perfectionistic or meticulous behavior	-.19	-.33
History of problematic substance (drug) abuse	.42	.36

Children Only:		
Child has difficulty getting to sleep	.28	.40

Females Only:	**Child**	**Adolescent**
Speech disturbance: Stuttering or stammering	-.28	-.23
Mother overly permissive, difficulty in setting limits	.35	.25

Correlate Placement:

>119T Runs away from home (32/65) [Adolescents only]
> History of problematic substance (alcohol) abuse (8/50)
>   [Male adolescents only]

>109T Truancy (17/73)
> Refer for psychiatric hospitalization (28/63)
> Involved with police (9/61)
> Poor prognosis for remediation of current problems (48/73) (DVL, ACH)
> Stealing (27/63) (HPR)
> Poor judgment/needs much supervision (47/75) [Adolescents only]
> Runs away from home (15/67) [Children only]
> Precocious sexual behavior or promiscuity (5/62) [Female adolescents only]
> History of problematic substance (drug) abuse (10/46) [Adolescents only]

>99T Father inconsistent in setting limits (39/67)
> Temper tantrums (37/66)
> Friends are mainly older than child (12/34)
> Described as being selfish (17/47) (HPR)
> [Mother inconsistent in setting limits (52/79)] (FAM)
> [Mother emotionally disturbed (in need of individual treatment) (39/57)] (FAM)
> Seems bright in many ways, but still achieves poorly in school (24/58) [Female adolescents only]
> Sleep disturbance: Awakens early (23/55) [Children only]
> (L)* Obsessive thought pattern (12/0) [Adolescents only]

Table 5-10 Continued (DLQ)
Correlate Placement:

> 89T Verbally hostile or argumentative (39/62)
       Expresses a dislike for school (28/57)
       [Disobedient to teachers or breaks school rules (42/63)] (HPR)
       (L) Refer for outpatient individual therapy (47/19) (PSY)
           [Male adolescents only]

> 79T Impulsive behavior (55/79) (HPR)
       Blames others for his/her problems (22/66) (HPR)
       Displays irresponsible behavior (31/61) (HPR)
       Lying (34/61) (HPR)
       Poor judgment/needs much supervision (15/67) [Children only]
       (L) Perfectionistic or meticulous behavior (18/4) [Adolescents only]

> 69T Disobedient to parents (34/73) (HPR)

< 60T (L) Running away from home (4/30)
       (L) Truancy (5/29)
       (L) Stealing (9/35)
       (L) Father inconsistent in setting limits (14/52)
       (L) Blames others for his/her problems (17/42)
       (L) Poor judgment/needs much supervision (18/57)
       (L) Temper tantrums (18/47)
       (L) Lying (23/52)
       (L) Mother inconsistent in setting limits (27/63)
       (L) Poor prognosis for remediation of current problems (23/55) (DLQ)

*Scale range suggests reduced frequency of correlate.

Table 5-10 documents the relationship between a variety of hostile, impulsive behaviors and DLQ elevation. Involvement with police, rejection of the school experience, and parental difficulty managing the child's behavior are reflected by elevations on DLQ. Internalizing behaviors are inversely related to scale elevation for adolescents only. Interpretive guidelines suggest that elevations >79T reflect impulsive, irresponsible behavior. With increasing elevation (>89T), difficulty controlling anger and difficulties in school are more likely. Antisocial behavior and substance abuse are more likely at elevations >109T. The analysis indicates a clear relationship between increasing scale elevation and the increased probability of significant antisocial behaviors, particularly for adolescents.

Table 5-11

Withdrawal Scale (WDL): Clinical Descriptors and Ratings

Total Sample:
       Isolative (usually plays alone, stays in room, etc.) (.34, .31)
       Excessive shyness   (.25, .25)
       Has few or no friends   (.24, .12)

Table 5-11 Continued (WDL)

Children Only:	Male	Female
Concrete thinking beyond age expectation	.25	.44
Frequently unresponsive to surroundings	.26	.39
Decreased verbal communication	.30	.36
Friends are mainly younger than child	.19	.38
Poor prognosis for remediation of current problems	.23	.39

Females Only:	Child	Adolescent
Speech disturbance: Phonation	.33	.39

Correlate Placement:

>79T Excessive shyness (19/41) (D, SSK)
   Frequently unresponsive to surroundings (18/50) [Children only]

>69T Isolative (usually plays alone, stays in room, etc.) (30/61) (D, PSY)
   Separation anxiety (6/26) (SOM) [Male children only]

<50T (L)* Isolative (usually plays alone, stays in room, etc.) (21/43) (D, PSY)

---

*Scale range suggests reduced frequency of correlate.

Few replicated correlates were found for WDL. Poor social skills and isolative behavior were suggested by WDL elevations.

Table 5-12

Anxiety Scale (ANX): Clinical Descriptors and Ratings

Total Sample:
   Isolative (usually plays alone, stays in room, etc.)   (.16, .21)
   Mother overly permissive, difficulty setting limits   (.21, .16)
   Sleep disturbance: Has nightmares/bad dreams   (.14, .30)

Children Only:	Male	Female
History of physical fights with peers	.23	.31

Correlate Placement:

>79T Mother overly permissive, difficulty in setting limits (37/63) (D)
   Perfectionistic or meticulous behavior (8/33) [Female children only]
   [Decreased appetite (9/27)] (D) [Female children only]

>69T Sleep disturbance: Has nightmares/bad dreams (23/40)

<50T (L)* Sleep disturbance: Has nightmares/bad dreams (11/32)

---

*Scale range suggests reduced frequency of correlate.

Table 5-13

Psychosis Scale (PSY): Clinical Descriptors and Ratings

Total Sample:

Isolative (usually plays alone, stays in room, etc.) (.32, .25)

Has few or no friends (.28, .24)

Sleep disturbance: Has difficulty getting to sleep (.25, .24)

Destructive of objects (.23, .25)

Overactive or agitated (.22, .22)

Functions at below average intellectual level (.22, .24)

Poor prognosis for remediation of current problems (.22, .21)

Abnormal motor behavior (spinning, hand flapping, gesturing, etc.) (.30, .20)

Speech disturbance:

  Phonation (.23, .18)

  Echolalia (.18, .22)

Poor judgment/needs much supervision (.19, .17)

Rapid mood shifts (.20, .16)

Concrete thinking beyond age expectation (.16, .29)

Expects rejection from others (.16, .15)

Self-destructive behavior (.13, .19)

Resistant to change in environment (.12, .19)

Described as being selfish (.11, .27)

Achievement in school at least on year below chronological age grade placement (underachievement) (.11, .15)

Children Only:	**Male**	**Female**
Displays expressive aphasic symptoms (unable to find words to express ideas; uses general or related word rather than specific word desired)	.21	.32
Sleep disturbance: Awakens early	.25	.35
Intentional enuresis: Continuing	.24	.36

Males Only:	**Child**	**Adolescent**
Recommendation for chemotherapy represents a change from current chemotherapy	.20	.22

Correlate Placement:

>109T Resistant to change in the environment (25/61)

  Abnormal motor behavior (spinning, hand flapping, gesturing, etc.) (3/28)

  Speech disturbance: Echolalia (1/17) (IS)

  [Overactive or agitated (26/61)] (HPR)

  [Speech disturbance: Phonation (6/33)] (ACH)

  Displays an associative (thought) disorder (2/29) [Male adolescents only]

> 99T Self-destructive behavior (wrist-slashing, head-banging, etc.) (13/26)

  Poor judgment/needs much supervision (50/74) (ACH)

  Sleep disturbance: Awakens early (23/55) [Children only]

Table 5-13 Continued (PSY)
Correlate Placement:

>89T Rapid mood shifts (sad or angry one day, happy the next) (43/67)
      Sleep disturbance: Has difficulty getting to sleep (27/53)
      Destructive of objects (31/58) (HPR)
      [Has few or no friends (46/70)] (SSK)
      [Isolative (usually plays alone, stay in room, etc.) (34/59)] (D, WDL)
      [Concrete thinking beyond age expectation (18/35)] (ACH, DVL)
      Easily upset or irritable (47/68) [Male children only]

>69T (L)* [Refer for outpatient individual therapy (46/25)] (DLQ)
          [Male adolescents only]

<50T (L) Destructive of objects (19/39)
      (L) Sleep disturbance: Has difficulty getting to sleep (7/35)
      (L) [Poor prognosis for remediation of current problems (17/54)] (DLQ)
      (L) [Isolative (usually plays alone, stays in room, etc.) (4/43)] (D, WDL)

---

*Scale range suggests reduced frequency of correlate.

Correlates for PSY reflect poor social relations, limited intellectual and academic skills, difficulty adapting to the environment, and symptoms associated with psychotic behavior (e.g., abnormal motor behavior, echo-lalia). Interpretive guidelines suggest that extreme elevations (>109T) reflect severe symptomatology while moderate elevations (90-108T) document isolative behavior, difficulty controlling affect, and poor judgment.

Table 5-14

Hyperactivity Scale (HPR): Clinical Descriptors and Ratings

Total Sample:
      Teases peers   (.41, .34)
      Disobedience to teachers or breaks school rules   (.34, .35)
      Lying   (.44, .31)
      History of physical fights with peers   (.35, .30)
      Overactive or agitated   (.28, .28)
      Disobedient to parents   (.27, .29)
      Complains of poor concentration/is easily distracted   (.25, .31)
      Often a poor sport and poor loser   (.36, .25)
      Overly controlling/bossy   (.24, .27)
      Displays irresponsible behavior   (.24, .32)
      Impulsive behavior   (.23, .40)
      Blames others for his/her problems   (.29, .23)
      Destructive of objects   (.24, .21)

Table 5-14 Continued (HPR)
Total Sample:
> Described as being selfish   (.28, .21)
> Complains of peer hostility and discrimination   (.20, .22)
> Unrealistic fears   (-.20, -.17)
> Seeks excessive approval   (.22, .18)
> Stealing   (.16, .25)
> Compulsive or ritualistic behavior   (-.18, -.14)
> Mother overly concerned or overly protective   (-.14, -.28)
> Biological parents currently divorced or separated   (.20, .13)

Adolescents Only:	**Male**	**Female**
Verbally hostile or argumentative	.28	.32
Poor prognosis for remediation of current problems	.23	.35

Children Only:		
Poor judgment/needs much supervision	.21	.38

Males Only:	**Child**	**Adolescent**
Somatic response to stress (e.g., stomachaches)	-.19	-.23
Previous psychotropic medication: Stimulants	.34	.28

Correlate Placement:

> 79T [Destructive of objects (34/59)] (PSY)
> > Chemotherapy indicated: Stimulants (35/88) [Male children only]

>69T Often a poor sport and poor loser (34/64) (SSK)
> History of physical fights with peers (33/61)
> Seeks excessive approval (36/55)
> Teases peers (19/53)
> Complains of peer hostility and discrimination (29/50)
> Overly controlling/bossy (14/32)
> (L)* Compulsive or ritualistic behavior (6/2)
> [Disobedient to parents (54/80)] (DLQ)
> [Blames others for his/her problems (30/60)] (DLQ)
> [Described as being selfish (18/38)] (DLQ)
> Seems bright in many ways, but still achieves poorly in school (42/63)
> > [Male adolescents only]
> (L) Overly conforming/passive follower (25/8) [Male adolescents only]

> 59T Complains of poor concentration/is easily distracted (34/66)
> (L) Unrealistic fears (31/15)
> (L) Maternal over concern or overprotection (44/23)
> Disobedient to teachers or breaks school rules (33/63) (DLQ)
> Overactive or agitated (13/41) (PSY)
> [Impulsive behavior (52/80)] (DLQ)
> [Lying (28/65)] (DLQ)
> [Displays irresponsible behavior (32/58)] (DLQ)
> [Stealing (19/43)] (DLQ)

Table 5-14 Continued (HPR)
Correlate Placement:

$<$40T (L) Overly controlling/bossy (4/21)
       (L) Teases peers (7/32)
       (L) Described as being selfish (8/26)
       (L) Disobedience to teachers or breaks school rules (12/55)
       (L) Displays irresponsible behavior (13/52)
       (L) Complains of poor concentration/is easily distracted (22/56)
       (L) Impulsive behavior (31/72)

---

*Scale range suggests reduced frequency of correlate.

Table 5-14 documents the relationship between HPR elevations and correlates suggestive of hyperactive behavior, poor peer relations, distractibility, and poor behavior controls. While both DLQ and HPR share a number or correlates, e.g., peer difficulties and dyscontrol, HPR correlates may reflect a different etiology for these overt behavior problems. These include: distractibility, poor concentration, and overactivity. DLQ correlates, on the other hand, suggest angry and antisocial behaviors as primary. Elevations $>$59T indicate the increased probability of school adjustment problems, distractibility, and overactivity. Poor peer relations are indicated at HPR elevations $>$69T.

Table 5-15

Social Skills Scale (SSK): Clinical Descriptors and Ratings

Total Sample:
       Has few or no friends   (.36, .34)
       Expects rejection from others   (.23, .42)
       Usually expects failure   (.21, .23)
       Isolative (usually plays alone, stays in room, etc.)   (.21, .23)
       Destructive of objects   (.17, .23)
       Excessive shyness   (.16, .26)
       Functions at below average intellectual level   (.16, .22)
       Chemotherapy indicated: Stimulants   (.17, .14)
       Overly critical of self   (.21, .13)
       Often a poor sport and poor loser   (.13, .23)

	Male	Female
Children Only:		
Disobedient to parents	.19	.40

	Child	Adolescent
Males Only:		
Previous psychotropic medication: Stimulants	.31	.22

Table 5-15 Continued (SSK)

Correlate Placement:

> 79T   Expects rejection from others (43/74)

> 69T   Has few or no friends (42/72) (PSY)
    [Often a poor sport and poor loser (36/50)] (HPR)
    [Overly critical of self (16/33)] (D)
    [Excessive shyness (16/31)] (D, WDL)

< 50T (L)* Has few or no friends (20/60)
    (L)   Expects rejection from others (17/52)
    (L)   Often a poor sport and poor loser (20/46)

---

*Scale range suggests reduced frequency of correlate.

SSK correlates document poor social relations, low self-esteem, and isolative behavior. Scale elevations > 69T reflect these behaviors.

CHAPTER 6

Interpretive Guidelines and Case Studies

This final chapter considers the practical application of the data presented in the previous three chapters. To achieve this end, proposed guidelines for the interpretation of profile scale elevations as well as comparisons between case histories and suggested PIC profile interpretations of six children and adolescents evaluated at the Lafayette Clinic are discussed.

Prior to a discussion of these applications, however, the authors feel it necessary to emphasize the limitations of the present study. Data presented here were collected at an urban child guidance facility, and the results can be applied with the most confidence to comparable populations. As indicated earlier, children or adolescents with suspected impaired cognitive functioning but without concommitant behavior problems were referred elsewhere. A limited number of subjects received diagnoses of mental retardation, psychosis, or psychophysiological disorder. Base rate occurrences of descriptive adjectives/symptoms clearly affect the statistical procedures employed. We suggest that our proposed specific guidelines may not be as accurate when applied in certain populations. Although the proposed interpretations may provide useful information and suggest areas for further investigation, utilization within institutions for the severely retarded and/or psychotic, or within a pediatric psychology service or a school psychology setting, may require extra caution. It is our hope that other investigators will study the validity of these PIC interpretations in a variety of clinical settings.

Proposed Interpretive Guidelines

Thirty-seven interpretive paragraphs were written for the PIC validity and clinical scales. These paragraphs reflect the integration of scale correlates documented in Chapters 3, 4, and 5. Figure 6-1 presents the PIC profile with the suggested interpretive ranges on each of the 16 scales. Each

T-score interval is numbered and corresponds to the interpretive paragraph number presented in the text below. The percentage beside each
paragraph indicates the proportion of the population included in the
T-score range for that particular scale. Suggested intervals range from
a minimum of one in scales L, DEF, and ADJ to a maximum of four on
scales DLQ and PSY.

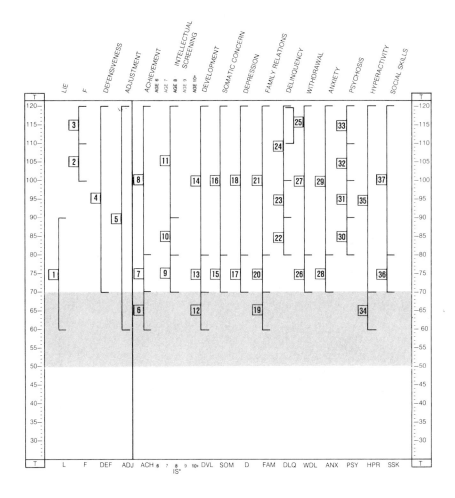

Figure 6—1
Suggested Interpretive T-Score Ranges for the PIC Profile Scales

Table 6-1

Proposed Interpretive Hypotheses for PIC Profile Scales

L >59T 8%	(1) Inventory responses suggest that the informant may have ascribed the most virtuous of behaviors and denied minor, commonly occurring behavior problems in the description of this child. This response set may have affected other scale elevations, such that the resulting profile interpretation may minimize current problems. Children seen for evaluation who obtain similar scores are less likely to be characterized by disobedient, aggressive, or anti-social behaviors.
F 100-109T 10%	(2) Several infrequent problems and symptoms are described in this protocol. These responses may indicate the presence of highly disruptive behaviors that may require hospitalization for their treatment.
F >109T 10%	(3) Many infrequent problems and symptoms are described in this protocol. These responses may indicate the presence of highly disruptive behaviors that may require hospitalization for their treatment. Similar response patterns may be obtained by informants who exaggerate child problems or who fail to respond to inventory items in a conventional manner. The possibilities of exaggeration and atypical response sets should be carefully excluded before credence is given to individual scale interpretations.
DEF >69T 10%	(4) This inventory was completed by an informant who may have been hesitant to describe problematic child behaviors and may be resistant to view existing behavior problems as caused by psychological or interpersonal factors. The resulting scale elevations may minimize existing problems.

Table 6-1 Continued

ADJ >59T 90%	(5) The description of this child's behavior suggests that a psychological/psychiatric evaluation may assist in the remediation of current problems.
ACH 60-69T 24%	(6) Inventory responses suggest the possibility of poor school performance and associated academic retardation. Teacher observation of limited concentration or difficulty in completion of classroom assignments may be associated with below age expectation performance in reading, mathematics, or spelling.
ACH 70-79T 21%	(7) Parents and teachers are likely to be concerned about this child's limited academic achievement. Teacher observation of distractibility or difficulty in completion of classroom assignments is suggested, as is retarded achievement in one or more skill areas. These may include: reading, mathematics, spelling, handwriting, and verbal expression. School history may include retention in grade to promote skill acquisition.
ACH >79T 13%	(8) A history of significant academic failure, and an associated negative self-image, is suggested. Similar children often approach school assignments with an "I can't do it" attitude; they give up easily, expect failure, or may withdraw into daydreaming. Inventory responses indicate poor academic performance, which may result in underdeveloped reading, mathematics, spelling, or handwriting abilities or in limited skills in verbal expression. A deficit in concentration and difficulty in completion of classroom assignments is likely. School history may include retention in grade to promote skill acquisition.

Table 6-1 Continued

IS 70-79T 13%	(9) Concern about limited intellectual endowment may be raised by a psychological evaluation. Poor school performance may be associated with an inability to retain and apply basic skills taught in previous grades.
IS 80-89T 9%	(10) The presence of intellectual deficits may be suggested by a psychological evaluation. Similar children are frequently described by their parents as acting younger than their chronological age and may be observed by their teachers to lack basic skills taught in previous classes. Preadolescents may display poor physical education skills. Adolescents may be troubled by nocturnal enuresis.
IS >89T 12%	(11) Reported child behavior and development suggests the need for a thorough intellectual assessment. Limitations in verbal, social, and perceptual-motor skills are likely to be noticed by parents, teachers, and peers. Similar children act younger than their chronological age, may be unconcerned about personal appearance, often are rejected by peers, and may seek friends among younger children. Preadolescents are likely to display poor physical education skills. Adolescents may be troubled by nocturnal enuresis.
DVL 60-69T 24%	(12) Teachers are likely to observe that this child is easily distracted away from the tasks at hand by ordinary classroom stimuli. Classroom performance may reflect poor study skills. A psychological/psychiatric evaluation may result in specific recommendations to school personnel.

Table 6-1 Continued

DVL 70-79T 17%	(13)	Clinical examination and teacher observation are likely to suggest deficits in motor coordination, language skills, or cognitive functions. Similar children may evidence fine or gross motor clumsiness or concrete thinking beyond age expectation. In interviews, they may display receptive or expressive aphasic symptoms. Speech may be described as limited or immature or characterized by poor articulation. Teachers may report poor performance in physical education activities or may observe difficulty in fine motor coordination, such as in drawing. Classroom performance may reflect poor study skills or difficulty in understanding instructions. A psychological/psychiatric evaluation may result in specific recommendations to school personnel.
DVL >79T 10%	(14)	Clinical examination and teacher observation are likely to suggest deficits in motor coordination, language skills, and cognitive functions. Parents may recall delayed development for this child in such skills as standing alone, learning to walk, or speaking first words. One or more problems with present speech may be noted by parents, teachers, and clinicians. Speech may be described as limited or immature or characterized by poor articulation or phonation. In interviews, these children may display receptive or expressive aphasic symptoms. Fine and gross motor clumsiness and concrete thinking beyond age expectation may be observed. Teachers may report poor performance in physical education activities or may observe difficulty in fine motor coordination, such as in drawing. Classroom performance may reflect poor study skills or difficulty in understanding instructions. Psychological/psychiatric evaluation often leads to specific recommendations to school personnel. If the child is currently in a regular classroom, the teacher may be considering the appropriateness of a special class placement.

Table 6-1 Continued

SOM 70-79T 19%	(15)	This child may complain of aches and pains. These somatic symptoms may be employed to avoid responsibilities or to withdraw from uncomfortable situations.
SOM >79T 32%	(16)	Health related complaints are likely to require professional attention. Sustained fatigue, aches and pains, or headaches may be present. A careful evaluation will be necessary to determine whether physical symptoms are employed to avoid responsibilities, are used to withdraw from uncomfortable situations, are in response to stress, accompany depression or other emotional states, and/or require medical intervention.
D 70-79T 22%	(17)	Similar children are often described as sad or unhappy. Their dispositions are often characterized by frequent mood changes which may occur without apparent cause. Frequent periods of crying or isolation may be characteristic.
D >79T 32%	(18)	This child's behavior is likely to reflect the presence of sadness and unhappiness. Depression may be indicated by problems with sleeping, eating, emotional lability, isolation, excessive worry, self-blame, or self-criticism. Among adolescents, these symptoms may be associated with suicidal thought and behavior.

Table 6-1 Continued

FAM 60-69T 28%	(19) The home is likely to reflect the impact of divorce or separation and may be characterized by instability and conflict. Parental inconsistency in setting limits is suggested. The resulting parent-child interaction may contribute to the development of child behavior problems.
FAM 70-79T 19%	(20) A history of marital discord as well as subsequent separation or divorce is suggested. One or both parents may be judged to require professional assistance to deal with their emotional instability, alcoholism, or substance abuse. Parental inconsistency in setting limits may contribute to the development of child behavior problems.
FAM >79T 7%	(21) A history of marital discord as well as subsequent separation or divorce is suggested. One or both parents may be judged to require professional assistance to deal with their emotional instability, alcoholism, or substance abuse. Child behavior problems may result from parenting characterized by inconsistency, undue criticism, rejection, or the use of excessive physical punishment.
DLQ 80-89T 17%	(22) Resistance to the requests of adults at home and in school is often indicated. Similar children are frequently described as impulsive by mental health professionals who may note irresponsible behavior, poor judgment, or an established tendency to blame others for current problems. A hostile, unsocialized orientation may be suggested by argumentativeness, lying, or stealing.

Table 6-1 Continued

DLQ 90-99T 14%	(23)	A disregard for rules and societal expectations is likely to be evidenced by behavior displayed at both home and school. Similar children may express a dislike for school and demonstrate a hostile, defiant response to school personnel. Current behavior is likely to reflect impulsivity, poor judgment, or unmodulated hostility. An antisocial adjustment may be suggested by such symptoms as lying, stealing, association with similar troubled children, or by an established tendency to blame others for current problems.
DLQ >99T 22%	(24)	A disregard for rules and societal expectations is likely to be evidenced by behavior displayed at home and at school. Similar children dislike school and demonstrate a poor academic adjustment associated with hostility and defiance or apathy and disinterest. Current behavior is likely to reflect impulsivity, poor judgment, or unmodulated hostility. A characterological disorder may be suggested by such symptoms as lying, stealing, problematic sexual behavior, group delinquent activities, or an established tendency to blame others for current problems.
DLQ >109T 15%	(25)	Law enforcement agencies may be aware of delinquent child behaviors, such as truancy, running away from home, or alcohol/drug abuse. Mental health professionals are likely to be pessimisitic about remediation of current problems and may feel that institutional treatment is indicated.

Table 6-1 Continued

WDL 70-79T 13%	(26) Inventory responses suggest the presence of social withdrawal. Similar children are described by their parents as playing alone most of the time and by their teachers as frequently avoiding group activities. Preadolescents may evidence anxiety when separated from their parents.
WDL >79T 19%	(27) Withdrawal and discomfort in social interactions are suggested. This child is likely to be described by both parents and teachers as excessively shy. Children with similar inventory scores are frequently isolative; they play alone, avoid group activities at school, and stay away from other family members at home. Preadolescents may be unresponsive to school surroundings and may evidence anxiety when separated from their parents.
ANX 70-79T 20%	(28) Child behavior may reflect fearfulness and worry. Presenting complaints may include troubled sleep, distrust of others, or multiple fears.
ANX >79T 16%	(29) Child behavior is likely to reflect significant fearfulness and worry. Presenting complaints frequently include trouble falling asleep, nightmares, distrust of others, fear of school, or an excessive need to avoid personal error. The mothers of these children may be seen as overly permissive and often have difficulty setting limits on child demands.

Table 6-1 Continued

PSY 80-89T 19%	(30)	This child may be socially isolated and emotionally labile. Parents may describe this child as "often confused or in a daze" and may note excessive daydreaming as well as other strange or peculiar behaviors.
PSY 90-99T 11%	(31)	This child's behavior is likely to be characterized by social isolation and emotional lability. Parents frequently describe similar children as "often confused or in a daze" and may note excessive daydreaming as well as other strange or peculiar behaviors.
PSY 100-109T 8%	(32)	This child's behavior is likely to be characterized by social isolation and emotional lability. Similar children are frequently described by their parents as "often confused or in a daze"; additional strange or peculiar behaviors may be noted. Excessive daydreaming or delayed motor and language developmental milestones may also be reported. Other problems may include self-destructive behavior (such as head-banging), destruction of objects, poor judgment, rapid mood shifts, difficulty getting to sleep, or early morning awakening. A psychological/psychiatric evaluation may determine whether these behaviors reflect a serious or progressive disability in empathic skills or thought processes.

Table 6-1 Continued

PSY >109T   (33) Current child behavior suggests serious psychologi-
6%   cal maladjustment that may be characterized by
                    unusual thoughts and behaviors, social isolation,
                    and emotional lability. Parents frequenty note that
                    similar children are "confused or in a daze" and
                    may note excessive daydreaming. Delayed develop-
                    mental milestones may be reported for social skills,
                    language ability, or motor coordination. Similar
                    children may be resistant to change in the environ-
                    ment, may display rapid mood shifts, or demon-
                    strate poor judgment. Self-destructive behavior
                    (such as head-banging), destruction of objects,
                    difficulty in getting to sleep, or early morning
                    awakening may be present. Current behaviors may
                    include symptoms that are frequently associated
                    with severe emotional disability, such as abnormal
                    motor behavior, echolalic speech, or an associative
                    thought disorder. Evaluation of this child's inter-
                    personal relations and thought processes may reflect
                    a pathological perception of reality.

HPR 60-69T   (34) Current child behavior may reflect a poor social and
26%   academic adjustment that is associated with over-
                    activity, distractibility, or provocation of peers.
                    Similar children are frequently described as restless,
                    fidgety, and inattentive in the classroom. They are
                    excessively social in school and may require adult
                    intervention to limit impulsive, disruptive, and
                    annoying behaviors. Demonstrating limited frus-
                    tration tolerance, such children frequently fight with
                    and pick on other children, break things, displace
                    anger, distrust others, or are described as poor
                    losers. Poor gross motor coordination or accident
                    proneness may be present.

Table 6-1 Continued

HPR > 69T 29%	(35) A history of problematic peer relations is suggested that may be characterized by poorly controlled expression of hostility, fighting, provocation and teasing, or poor sportsmanship. Current and/or past behavior may also suggest hyperactivity, distractibility, restlessness, or impulsivity. Similar children are often inattentive in class, do not complete homework assignments, and may require adult intervention to conform to stated limits. A limited frustration tolerance may be associated with temper tantrums, destruction of objects, projection of blame, direct expression or displacement of anger, or a lack of trust in others. Other problems may include excessive seeking of attention and approval, clumsiness, frequent accidents, or fire-setting.
SSK 70-79T 26%	(36) This child is likely to have difficulty making and keeping friends. Similar children may not initiate relationships with peers and are often unskilled at the mutual give-and-take of play. Social isolation or conflict may result.
SSK >79T 21%	(37) A history of poor peer relations may lead this child to expect criticism and rejection from others. Parents and teachers frequently observe that similar children have few, if any, friends. Poor social skills may be demonstrated by a failure to initiate relationships, with resulting isolation, or by conflict with peers that reflects poor sportsmanship and limited frustration tolerance.

The interpretive paragraphs reflect both descriptor/correlates to scale elevation and criterion source. Thus, inspection of the paragraphs reveals descriptors provided by parents, teachers, or clinicians at various T-score ranges. The paragraphs suggested for DLQ (22 through 25) will serve as an illustrative example. As Figure 6-1 indicates, paragraph 22 is suggested for scale scores between 80-89T. Correlates for this T-score range, as well as the obtained criterion frequency below and above the cutting score have been presented in Tables 3-11, 4-8, and 5-10. Within the 80-89T range, resistance to requests of adults and teachers is likely. Clinicians tend to ascribe impulsivity, poor judgment, and a tendency to project blame for difficulties. All three criterion sources indicate an unsocialized orientation, as evidenced by stealing, lying, and argumentativeness. Paragraph 23 (90-99T) includes the descriptors suggested for scale scores 80-89T with additional references to defiance to instructions and expressed dislike for school noted by school personnel and clinicians, while parents note that involvement with other troubled children is likely. It is important to recognize that correlates selected at >79T and used to generate paragraph 22 are descriptive of all scale scores above this cut-off point. Further, the accuracy of prediction of criterion presence often increases with higher scale elevation. For this reason, statements were written to reflect these changing statistics. Thus, when referring to resistance to parents and teachers, the paragraph indicates these behaviors are "often indicated" (80-89T), "likely to be evidenced" (90-99T), and "evidenced by" (>99T). For further clarification, the reader is referred to Appendices B and C which detail correlate frequency within T-score intervals.

The interpretive paragraphs indicate age specific descriptors where appropriate, by including correlates of limited generalizability that were significantly related to scale elevation. The terms "adolescent" (>12 yrs) and "preadolescent" (≤12 yrs) limit these expected behaviors and descriptors. Exceptions to this procedure are found in paragraphs 24 and 25 for scale DLQ. Although Table 5-10 indicates a number of adolescent-specific correlates, it was felt unnecessary to qualify these interpretive statements as 85% of the protocols in our sample with DLQ T-score >99T were generated as descriptions of adolescents. The reader should note that for scale scores >109T on DLQ (see Figure 6-1) paragraphs 24 *and* 25 are applicable. General interpretive statements are suggested for the profile validity scales (paragraphs one through five) which reflect the replicated correlates for the total sample. As the *Manual* (Wirt et al., 1977) indicates, these scales were constructed to help identify response sets that may have influenced the accuracy and therefore interpretation of the clinical scales. While this study did not investigate the ability of the validity scales to predict deviant response sets, paragraphs also include cautionary state-

ments regarding validity that are derived from the intent for which the
scale was developed. It is our hope that other investigators will study the
relationship between deviant response sets and validity scales in a variety
of populations. The need to identify invalid protocols based on F scale
elevation, for example, has import in both clinical *and* research areas.
Similarly, it is clinically important to note protocols in which it is likely
that the informant has minimized the child's emotional disturbance.

Profile Interpretation

It is suggested that profile interpretation proceed on a content-oriented
basis, grouping scales that tap similar and/or related phenomena. Our
current preference is to group profile scales into three content domains:

1) General adjustment (ADJ) and informant response style (L, F, DEF)
2) Cognitive development (IS, DVL) and academic performance (ACH)
3) Personality (SOM, D, DLQ, WDL, ANX, PSY, HPR, SSK) and
   family evaluation (FAM)

General adjustment and informant response style. The clinician's first
effort is to evaluate validity and screening scale elevations because they
provide information as to the accuracy of the remaining profile scales.
Significant elevations of L and DEF suggest denial of common behavioral
difficulties and minimization of existing problems. If significant elevations
are present, caution is suggested in profile interpretation as is the need for
careful investigation into possible sources of informant defensiveness.
Cases with L or DEF elevations may include, for example, referrals initiated by courts or educational institutions with which the parental informant is not in agreement.

Elevations on ADJ (>59T) suggest that a psychological or psychiatric
evaluation is indicated. Fully 90% of our sample fell above this suggested
cut-off. T-scores <60T are not indicative of atypical intellectual, academic, or emotional status, although the remaining PIC scales should be
reviewed to substantiate this conclusion.

Finally, F scale elevations >99T reflect behaviors of a disruptive,
serious nature. With scale scores >109T, the clinician should also entertain the possibility of informant exaggeration of difficulties or atypical
response sets.

Cognitive development and academic performance. As intellectual
functioning affects the child's ability to adequately cope with the demands
of his or her environment (academic, social, and interpersonal), it is suggested that IS be the first clinical scale evaluated. Significant elevation on
IS suggests impaired cognitive functioning that may have contributed to
the child's present difficulties as reflected by other profile scale elevations.

DVL elevations which are indicative of poor study skills, fine or gross motor clumsiness, and speech and language difficulties should then be examined, followed by ACH. Elevations on IS and DVL suggest possible explanations for poor academic achievement. If ACH is elevated, but IS and DVL are not, the clinician might entertain other hypotheses for poor school performance (e.g., lack of motivation, emotional disturbance).

Personality and family functioning. Our order of preference in the third content domain involves an estimate of social skills (SSK), emotional lability, and serious or progressive disability in empathic skills or thought processes (PSY), internalizing behaviors (WDL, D, ANX, SOM), poor behavioral or impulse control (DLQ and HPR), and finally an estimate of family intactness and effectiveness (FAM).

Examples of PIC Interpretation

In this section the histories of six behaviorally or emotionally disturbed children have been abstracted from intake evaluations completed at Lafayette Clinic. The case history material is followed by the notation on the PIC profile form of suggested interpretations. These interpretations are then compared with the relevant intake data.

Case History 1. This 10-year-old Caucasian male was brought to the clinic for an evaluation by his parents. His mother stated that she had difficulty getting him to do his homework or household chores. He had problems learning in school and had been placed in a special education classroom for the educable mentally retarded after the first grade. Teachers reported that he was restless and fidgety, did not pay attention in class, daydreamed, stayed in school halls for long periods of time, and didn't seem interested in interacting with peers. At times he quarreled with peers. His mother stated that she did not allow him to play with peers at home for fear that he might associate with a "bad crowd."

His mother also reported that she and her son shared the same bed. At times he complained of nightmares and a fear of monsters and had been physically comforted by his mother. She had not attempted toilet training and stated that her son frequently wet the bed.

This child's parents did not marry until two years after his birth. The father was described as an alcoholic who was uninvolved in the family. He frequently left the home in the morning and did not return until late at night.

This child was a full-term baby and was delivered by Cesarean section. His birth weight was 5 lbs. 4 oz. Developmental milestones were within normal limits, although fine and gross motor skills were impaired. He could not, for example, tie his shoes until the age of eight. Physical examination was within normal limits. The neurological examination suggested that all reflexes were hyperactive.

A cognitive and perceptual motor screening completed on the day of the psychiatric evaluation suggested impairment in verbal skills and visual-motor coordination. While pragmatic problem-solving skills were good, difficulties with impulse control were noted.

Figure 6-2 presents the PIC profile for Case History 1. Inspection of this profile indicates that seven scales suggest interpretive hypotheses. The numbers placed at scale elevations indicate the appropriate interpretive paragraph.

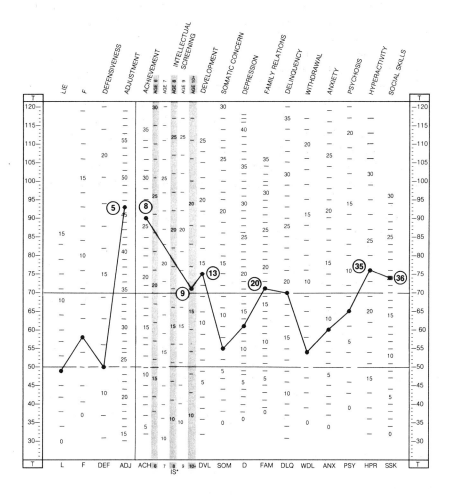

Figure 6—2
PIC Profile: Case History 1

Comparison of the PIC paragraphs with the case history material suggests that the PIC clearly predicted concern over limited intellectual abilities, poor study skills, fine and gross motor problems, and academic retardation. Further, poor peer relationships were indicated as well as dyscontrol, inattentiveness in class, impulsivity, and problems conforming to limits. Finally, problematic family relations were also suggested by the FAM T-score elevation. Employing the guidelines suggested, however, the PIC failed to predict the nightmares and fearfulness described by the mother, suggesting that symptoms may have been manipulative in nature.

Case History 2. This six-year-old black male resided with his father, stepmother, and two stepsiblings. His mother related that he had a past history of hyperactivity and had had a positive response to treatment with methylphenidate. Medication had been discontinued, however, for the past five months. His stepmother, of the past two years, reported a history of extreme activity, distractibility, impulsivity, and behavior problems in nursery school. He fought with other children and did not respond to limit setting by teachers. He was described as a poor sleeper, extremely irritable, and would frequently lie to his parents, particularly about negative behaviors at school. Physical punishment appeared to have no effect on his behavior. His stepmother knew little of this child's birth or early development other than that toilet training was difficult and not completed until age three.

School personnel described this child as displaying a poor attention span, distractibility, impulsivity, and noted that he failed to complete assignments.

Physical and neurological examination suggested some difficulty with finger-to-nose coordination. Sensory and motor functions appeared grossly intact. Psychometric assessment suggested average intellectual abilities. No specific areas of deficiency were noted other than an impulsive style of responding.

The PIC profile describing this child is presented in Figure 6-3. Three scales, ADJ, ACH, and HPR, fall within interpretable ranges.

Interpretive paragraphs accurately reflected concerns expressed by this child's stepmother and teachers. This particular case history documented the effectiveness of HPR in predicting overactivity, distractibility, and impulsiveness noted by teachers.

Case History 3. This six-year-old black female was attending the first grade. Her parents had been separated for five months. Her mother noted that this girl had been forgetful, recently losing her shoes and articles of clothing. She was sullen and quiet at home and had been fighting more with her older sister. Her father, on the other hand, did not report sullen,

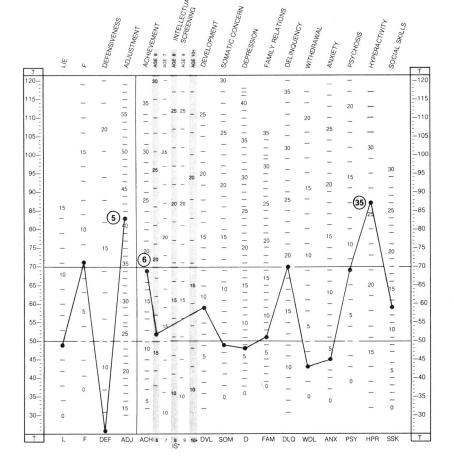

Figure 6—3
PIC Profile: Case History 2

withdrawn behavior when she was with him. She had experienced night-mares at home, which appeared to be related to difficulties between her parents. Her parents agreed that her problems increased after their separation.

This child was a full-term infant with no difficulties during delivery or following birth. Developmental milestones were unremarkable. Her mother, however, stated that throughout the pregnancy she had night-mares about giving birth to a "monster." She noted that she had been very upset and anxious after the birth, fearful that something would happen to the child, and was overprotective as a result.

She had been doing average work in school, although her work was sloppy and seldom completed. She became upset and cried whenever she did not do well. Some difficulty with concentration and following instructions was also reported.

The physical and neurological examinations were within normal limits. Psychological screening confirmed the absence of specific areas of intellectual deficit.

Figure 6-4 presents the PIC profile for this child.

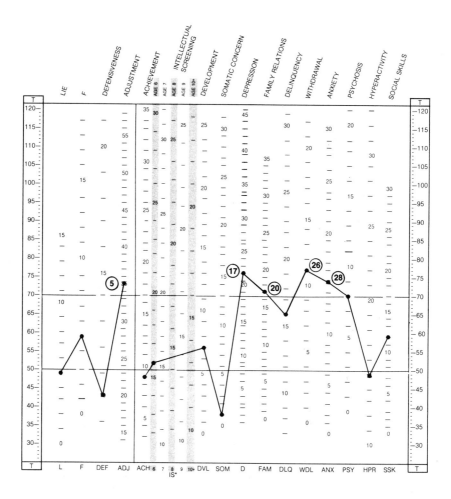

Figure 6—4
PIC Profile: Case History 3

Three of the four elevated clinical scales suggested internalizing behaviors. More specifically, scale elevations suggested the presence of social withdrawal, sadness or unhappiness, fearfulness, and troubled sleep. These scale interpretations were consistent with the concerns expressed by this mother. Further, marital discord and conflict were reflected by the FAM elevation.

Case History 4. The parents of this 15-year-old Caucasian female initiated the referral to the clinic. Over the preceding three weeks she had become increasingly withdrawn and irritable, cried all the time, had a tendency toward excessive sleeping, and was generally disinterested in her surroundings. These symptoms occurred at the time of her proposed entry into a school sorority which involved a number of degrading and humiliating experiences. The current evaluation documented problem areas which led to subsequent hospitalization. Three episodes of a similar nature had occurred previously. Once at age nine, while on a camping trip with the entire family, and another two winters ago, at camp. Both episodes subsided with her return home. The third occurrence had taken place approximately 18 months previously. School personnel noted that she had been extremely withdrawn and had acted rather bizarrely, even to the point of lying on the floor in the classroom. She had been seen by a psychiatrist at that time and placed on thioridazine which resulted in rapid improvement and symptom resolution.

Information from the school indicated that no significant academic problems were present. Parents reported that she was a high achiever, although she tended to worry needlessly about tests.

This adolescent was born one month prematurely, but there were no problems with pregnancy or delivery. Developmental milestones were unremarkable. Physical and neurological examinations were within normal limits. Psychological testing indicated a Verbal IQ of 111, a Performance IQ of 102 and a Full Scale IQ of 107. Achievement testing demonstrated grade level performance.

Figure 6-5 presents the PIC profile generated by this adolescent's mother.

The suggested interpretive paragraphs indicated social withdrawal, depressive symptomatology, emotional lability, fearfulness, and a need to avoid personal error. The behavior patterns exhibited by this adolescent girl were predicted by the PIC scale elevations. Additionally, the relatively low scale scores on DLQ and HPR suggested that interpersonal difficulties of a hostile defiant nature were unlikely. The case history material supported this interpretation.

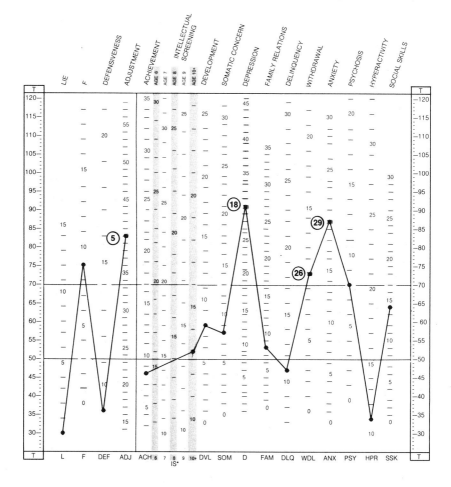

Figure 6—5
PIC Profile: Case History 4

Case History 5. This 15-year-old Caucasian male resided with his step-father and mother. His mother reported that approximately six years ago her son went to live with his father and stepmother. He remained there until age 13. During this time he expressed unhappiness with the home situation and experienced some academic failure. Upon return to his mother's home he became involved in a number of delinquent activities. These included auto theft, lying, stealing, disregard of maternal limit setting, and association with a delinquent group. He also threatened sui-cide as well as harm to other family members. Eight months previously he left home to reside with his aunt, at which time he began drinking and became argumentative. Police became involved when he threatened his aunt. This patient also reported use of marijuana and THC on infrequent occasions.

Pregnancy and delivery were unremarkable as were developmental milestones. Regressive nocturnal enuresis was problematic from age four to nine. Both the patient and his mother attributed this to concurrent marital strife. The natural father was described as an alcoholic and physically abusive. This mother was also described as a heavy drinker.

Reports from school indicated that the patient received average marks in all subjects except history.

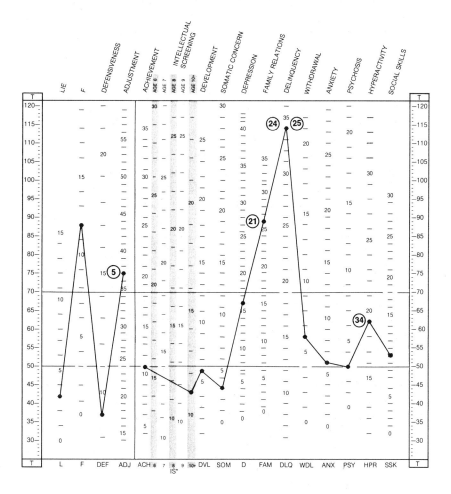

Figure 6—6
PIC Profile: Case History 5

His mother completed the PIC; the resulting profile is presented in Figure 6-6.

Correlates suggested by PIC scale elevations accurately predicted the historical data. These included this male adolescent's disregard for societal expectations, unmodulated hostility directed toward others, lying, stealing, alcohol abuse, involvement with police officials, and group delinquent activities. Paragraphs also suggested behavior difficulties in the classroom, such as restlessness, overactivity, and disruptive behaviors. Unfortunately, historical information, except for academic achievement, was minimal. The PIC scales, however, supported school information in that intellectual or academic functioning was not viewed as problematic. Finally, marital discord and the suggestion of emotional instability were indicated by the FAM elevations. As discussed earlier, this extreme elevation suggests that the clinician should investigate the role of family functioning in the etiology of behavior problems.

Case History 6. This 12-year-old black male was living with his maternal grandparents, who had legal custody since his birth. His biological mother was described as having both intellectual and emotional impairments. His father was an alcoholic who had died several years earlier. His grandmother stated that his difficulties were long-standing and that he had been very hyperactive six years prior to this evaluation, at which time he was placed on methylphenidate. He apparently improved for about five years, and the medication was discontinued. During the past year, however, he had become disruptive in class, engaged in multiple fist fights, tested his teachers, displayed temper tantrums, and displayed rapid mood swings. Additionally, he had difficulty relating to peers, and teachers described him as having few or no friends. Teachers also noted that he was observed to utter nonsense syllables and to babble. His grandmother stated that he had problems falling asleep, was easily disorganized, and was impulsive. The Mental Status Examination indicated pressure of speech, loose associations, and paranoid trends. He expressed concerns about tape recorders and their relation to himself. He also compared himself to a PT boat and a fighter pilot in World War II. He stated that he had dreams about castration and about having so many affairs with women that bodily injury would result. Depression was noted, particularly when he talked of his parents. The report also stated that he appeared quite anxious.

This patient was a product of a full-term gestation. No complications were noted, and developmental milestones were within normal limits. Psychological testing indicated a Verbal IQ of 77, a Performance IQ of 68, and a Full Scale IQ of 70. Achievement testing suggested variable skills. Grade levels ranged from 2.4 in mathematics to 6.4 on general information.

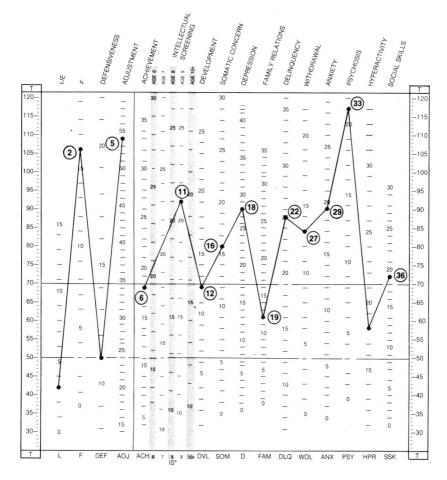

Figure 6—7
PIC Profile: Case History 6

Figure 6-7 presents the PIC generated by the maternal grandmother.
F scale elevation suggested infrequent child problems and behaviors that were substantiated by the history. An interpretation of the PIC utilizing the proposed paragraphs becomes quite lengthy because all but three scales (L, DEF, and HPR) fall within the suggested interpretive ranges. Our experience has indicated that this is not unlikely with extreme elevations on PSY. The reader is referred to the suggested interpretive ranges presented in Figure 6-1. This figure documents that clinically significant T-scores are not consistent across scales. Furthermore, it will be noted that the most pathological description on PSY is reserved for elevations >109T.

With D elevations, depressive symptomatology is maximally predicted by T-scores >79T. Given this phenomenon, it would seem appropriate that the clinician take into account not only absolute scale elevation in his interpretation, but also the relative importance of individual scale elevations. For example, examination of the profile presented in Figure 6-7 indicates that elevations on IS, SOM, D, WDL, ANX, and PSY represent extreme T-scores on the individual scales. On the other hand, T-scores on ACH, DVL, FAM, DLQ, and SSK fall within the lowest interpretive ranges. This approach suggests that emphasis be on IS, PSY, WDL, D, ANX, and SOM elevations in the interpretation of the profile. A suggested interpretation employing this strategy is presented below:

This informant's description of this child's behavior suggests that a psychological/psychiatric evaluation may assist in the remediation of current difficulties. Infrequent problems and symptoms have been ascribed to the child and suggest highly disruptive behaviors that may require hospitalization for treatment. The possibilities of exaggeration and atypical response sets should be carefully excluded.

Limitations in verbal, social, and perceptual-motor skills are likely to be noticed by parents, teachers, and peers, and the need for a thorough intellectual assessment is indicated.

Teachers are likely to observe distractibility, poor study skills, and academic retardation in reading, mathematics, or spelling. Similar children act younger than their chronological age, may be unconcerned about personal appearance, and are often rejected by peers. An evaluation may result in specific recommendations to school personnel.

Current behavior suggests serious psychological maladjustment, which may be characterized by unusual thoughts and behaviors, social isolation, and emotional lability. Similar children demonstrate self-destructive behavior, destruction of objects, difficulty getting to sleep, or early morning awakening. Abnormal motor behavior, echolalic speech, or an associative thought disorder may be present.

Problematic withdrawal and discomfort in social interactions are suggested. Significant sadness and unhappiness are indicated as well as fearfulness and worry. Health-related complaints are likely and may be evidenced by sustained fatigue, aches and pains, or headaches.

The home is likely to reflect the impact of divorce or separation and may be characterized by instability or conflicts.

The paragraphs suggested by IS, SOM, D, WDL, ANX, and PSY clearly described the presenting symptomatology. Psychological testing indicated the accuracy of IS's prediction of the need for an intellectual assessment and difficulties in peer relationships. PSY reflected the serious psychological maladjustment he evidenced, including social isolation, emotional lability, aggressive/destructive behavior, and a thought disorder. WDL, D, ANX, and SOM predicted internalizing behaviors documented in the history. It is interesting to note that the initial evaluation focused primarily on behaviors of an externalizing nature, although significant depression and anxiety were suggested. Due to the severity of his disturbance, he was hospitalized. A trial of methylphenidate increased symptoms of a thought disorder, while thioridazine and haloperidol caused sedation with little or no symptomatic improvement. During hospitalization the affective component of his difficulties became more apparent, and he was placed on a trial of lithium carbonate. Marked improvement was noted, and he was later discharged to outpatient care. Although many of the adjectives used in the history suggested hyperactivity, elevation of HPR did not reach an interpretive cut-off. This should suggest to the clinician that agitation, rather than a "hyperkinetic syndrome," was the source of these difficulties.

With use of the interpretive guidelines suggested by this study, it will become apparent to the clinician that lengthy reports are possible. Depending upon scale elevation and configuration, duplicative descriptors are also quite possible. For example, statements indicative of poor peer relations are suggested for elevations on IS, SSK, PSY, WDL, DLQ, and HPR. Similarly, poor academic achievement is predicted by a number of scale elevations. The sample PIC interpretation represents an integration of descriptors by content area, thereby eliminating repetitive statements. This procedure would be the most useful when a number of scales fall within interpretive ranges and tap similar dimensions of behavior.

A final, cautionary note should be made concerning the interpretation of the PIC profile. It would be desirable to be able to delineate the causal relationships between the descriptors predicted by scale elevations. One may be tempted, for example, to interpret FAM elevations as *causing* some of the other suggested symptoms. It is our view that this sort of interpretation, without additional supportive non-PIC data, is premature at this time and that additional clinical and research activity will be necessary before such statements can be made with confidence. At the present time, scale elevations should be viewed as suggesting areas for further clinical investigation. Evaluation of code type classification strategies, now in progress, may lead to a clarification of this issue.

REFERENCES

Achenbach, T.M. The classification of children's psychiatric symptoms: a factor-analytic study. *Psychological Monographs,* 1966, *80,* 1-37 (7, Whole No. 615).

Boerger, A. R., Graham, J. R., and Lilly, R. S. Behavioral correlates of single-scale MMPI code types. *Journal of Consulting and Clinical Psychology,* 1974, *42,* 398-402.

Darlington, R. B., and Bishop, C. H. Increasing test validity by considering inter-item correlations. *Journal of Applied Psychology,* 1966, *50,* 322-330.

DeHorn, A. Profile classification of children and adolescents on the Personality Inventory for Children and related empirical correlates (Doctoral dissertation, Wayne State University, 1977). *Dissertation Abstracts International,* 1977, *38,* (5-B), 2358.

DeHorn, A., Lachar, D., and Gdowski, C.L. Profile classification strategies for the Personality Inventory for Children. *Journal of Consulting and Clinical Psychology,* 1979, *47,* 874-881.

Gdowski, C. L. Dimensions of childhood psychopathology: Patterns of internalizing and externalizing symptomatology in hospitalized children. Unpublished Masters Thesis, Wayne State University, 1975.

Gdowski, C. L. Typologies of childhood psychopathology and their relationship with the Personality Inventory for Children. (Doctoral dissertation, Wayne State University, 1977). *Dissertation Abstracts International,* 1978, *38,* 5566-B.

Gdowski, C.L., Lachar, D., & Butkus, M. A methodological consideration in the construction of actuarial interpretation systems. *Journal of Personality Assessment,* 1980, *44,* 427-432.

Group for the Advancement of Psychiatry. *Psychopathological disorders in childhood: Theoretical considerations and a proposed classification.* New York: The Authors, 1966.

Gynther, M.D. White norms and black MMPIs: A prescription for discrimination? *Psychological Bulletin,* 1972, *28,* 173-179.

Gynther, M. D., Lachar, D., and Dahlstrom, W. G. Are special norms for minorities needed? Development of an MMPI F scale for blacks. *Journal of Consulting and Clinical Psychology,* 1978, *56,* 1403-1408.

Knobloch, H., and Pasamanick, B. (Eds.) *Gesell and Amatruda's developmental diagnosis: The evaluation and management of normal and abnormal neuropsychologic development in infancy and early childhood.* Hagerstown, Maryland: Harper and Row, 1974.

Lachar, D. *The MMPI: Clinical assessment and automated interpretation.* Los Angeles: Western Psychological Services, 1974.

Lachar, D., and Alexander, R. S. Veridicality of self-report: Replicated correlates of the Wiggins MMPI content scales. *Journal of Consulting and Clinical Psychology,* 1978, *46,* 1349-1356.

Lachar, D., Butkus, M., and Hryhorczuk, L. Objective personality assessment of children: An exploratory study of the Personality Inventory for Children (PIC) in a child psychiatric setting. *Journal of Personality Assessment*, 1978, *42*, 529-537.

Lachar, D., and Gdowski, C. L. Behavior problem factor correlates of the Personality Inventory for Children profile scales. *Journal of Consulting and Clinical Psychology*, 1979, *47*, 39-48.

Lapouse, R., and Monk, M. A. Behavior deviations in a representative sample of children: variations by sex, age, race, social class, and family size. *American Journal of Orthopsychiatry*, 1964, *34*, 436-446.

Meehl, P. E., and Rosen, A. Antecedent probability and the efficiency of psychometric signs, patterns, or cutting scores. *Psychological Bulletin*, 1955, 194-216.

Quay, H. C., and Quay, L. C. Behavior problems in early adolescence. *Child Development*, 1965, *36*, 215-220.

Sechrest, L. Incremental validity: a recommendation. *Educational and Psychological Measurement*, 1963, *23*, 153-158.

Walker, H. M. *Walker Problem Behavior Identification Checklist manual.* Los Angeles: Western Psychological Services, 1970.

Werry, J. S., and Quay, H. C. The prevalence of behavior symptoms in younger elementary school children. *American Journal of Orthopsychiatry*, 1971, *41*, 136-143.

Wirt, R. D., Lachar, D., Klinedinst, J. K., and Seat, P. D. *Multidimensional description of child personality: A manual for the Personality Inventory for Children.* Los Angeles: Western Psychological Services, 1977.

Appendix A
Pre-Appointment Information Form
Teacher Rating and School Information Form
Description of Current Problem Behaviors Form

LAFAYETTE CLINIC
DIVISION OF CHILD AND ADOLESCENT PSYCHIATRY
951 E. Lafayette
Detroit, Michigan 48207

PRE-APPOINTMENT INFORMATION

SEQUENCE NO.

C	1	0	1			
1			4	6		9

CHILD'S NAME: First   Middle   Last

11   30

SEX ☐ M ☐ F   32

BIRTHDATE   /   /   19
34   43

PARENT'S OR GUARDIAN'S NAME

STREET NO. AND NAME

CITY AND STATE   ZIP CODE   HOME TELEPHONE   BUSINESS TELEPHONE

REFERRAL SOURCE AND ADDRESS

FORM MAILED   /   /   19

We would like to obtain some information from you about this child's development and present problems in order to provide the best possible evaluation. This questionnaire is to be filled out by the child's mother or other person who can best describe the child's present problems. Please answer the questions about **only the child named above.** Be as accurate as possible; you may ask for assistance from any other family members who know your child.

In addition, two "Release of Information" forms have been enclosed. If your child has attended school, please complete items #1 — #6 on **both** "Release of Information" forms and return them to Lafayette Clinic along with this completed pre-appointment form in the envelope provided. These "Release of Information" forms will allow us to obtain necessary information from your child's school. Once we have received this completed form **and** the information from the school, your request for an evaluation will be promptly considered.

Thank you,

Intake Secretary
Telephone:

DMH-1-779-P

C	1	0	2
1			4

First, we would like you to answer **all** of the questions on this page to tell us about your child's development. Place an 'X' in the yes or no column for each item. Some questions require an approximate age or another number; please feel free to ask other relatives to assist you.

PREGNANCY   During the pregnancy, did this child's mother:

	Yes	No	Col		Yes	No	Col
Have German measles?			11	Have any severe emotional problems?			18
Have anemia? (low iron)			12	Have any vaginal infection, discharge, or bleeding?			19
Have diabetes?			13	Has this child's mother ever experienced a miscarriage?			20
Have any kidney problems?			14	Was the miscarriage from: last pregnancy **before** this child?			21
Use any drugs or medicine?			15	: next pregnancy **after** this child?			22
Have high blood pressure?			16	: any other pregnancy?			23
Have a high fever (103 or higher for 3 days or more)			17				

BIRTH

	Hours				Pounds	Ounces	
About how long was this child's mother in labor?		25 – 27		How much did the baby weigh at birth?	29 – 30	32 – 33	

	Yes	No	Col		Yes	No	Col
Was anesthetic used during delivery?			35	Were there any injuries to the baby at birth?			39
Did the baby have any problems breathing at birth?			36	Was an operation performed to deliver the baby?			40
Did the baby need blood at birth?			37	Were any instruments used to deliver the baby?			41
Was the baby placed in an incubator?			38	Did the baby have yellow jaundice at birth?			42

MEDICAL HISTORY   Has your child ever had the following:

	Yes	No	Col			Yes	No	Col
Measles?			44		Asthma?			52
Mumps?			45		Blow on the head?			53
Chicken pox?			46		High fever (104 or higher for 3 days or more)?			54
Scarlet fever?			47		Difficulty in sucking?			55
Rheumatic fever?			48		Seizures or convulsions?			56
Allergies to food?			49		Anemia (low iron or sickle cell)?			57
Other allergies?			50		Repeated or prolonged hospitalization?			58
Spells of vomiting?			51					

C	1	0	3
1			4

DEVELOPMENT   At about what age did your child first:

	Years	Months	Columns
Sit up?			11 – 14
Crawl?			16 – 19
Stand alone?			21 – 24
Walk by self?			26 – 29
Feed self?			31 – 34
Dress self? (except for buttoning or tying knots)			36 – 39
Speak first real words?			41 – 44
Speak first real sentences?			46 – 49
Become completely toilet trained?			51 – 54
Help with household tasks?			56 – 59
Ride a tricycle?			61 – 64
Ride a bicycle?			66 – 69
Tie own shoes?			71 – 74

We now would like you to tell us about your child's **current** problem(s). Please place an 'X' on one number for each problem listed, telling how long it has been a problem.

EXAMPLE: A child is in the 4th grade and has always done poorly in school, but is not afraid to go to school. The item would then be X'ed out like this:

		C	1	0	4

		Not a Problem	Less Than 6 Months	6 Months to 1 year	1 to 2 Years	More Than 2 years	Columns
EXAMPLE	Has problem learning in school	1	2	3	4	X	
	Is afraid to go to school	X	2	3	4	5	
PROBLEMS WITH EATING AND SLEEPING	Doesn't eat right	1	2	3	4	5	11
	Refuses to go to bed	1	2	3	4	5	12
	Trouble falling asleep	1	2	3	4	5	13
	Nightmares	1	2	3	4	5	14
	Wakes up very early	1	2	3	4	5	15
PHYSICAL PROBLEMS	Doesn't speak well	1	2	3	4	5	17
	Not fully toilet trained (wet bed, soils, etc.)	1	2	3	4	5	18
	Tired most of the time	1	2	3	4	5	19
	Has aches and pains	1	2	3	4	5	20
	Clumsy or accident prone	1	2	3	4	5	21
	Fakes being sick	1	2	3	4	5	22
SCHOOL PROBLEMS	Has problems learning in school	1	2	3	4	5	24
	Is afraid to go to school	1	2	3	4	5	25
	Won't obey school rules	1	2	3	4	5	26
	Often skips school	1	2	3	4	5	27
RELATIONSHIPS WITH OTHER CHILDREN	Picks on other children	1	2	3	4	5	29
	Has few or no friends	1	2	3	4	5	30
	Is picked on by other children	1	2	3	4	5	31
	Plays alone most of the time	1	2	3	4	5	32
	Fights with other children	1	2	3	4	5	33
	Has sex play with other children	1	2	3	4	5	34

Category	Item	1	2	3	4	5	
BEHAVIOR PROBLEMS	Uses drugs	1	2	3	4	5	37
	Runs away from home	1	2	3	4	5	38
	Lies	1	2	3	4	5	39
	Steals	1	2	3	4	5	40
	Sets fires	1	2	3	4	5	41
	Breaks things	1	2	3	4	5	42
SOCIAL SKILLS	Afraid of many things	1	2	3	4	5	44
	Very shy	1	2	3	4	5	45
	Poor loser	1	2	3	4	5	46
	Demands too much attention	1	2	3	4	5	47
OTHER PROBLEMS WITH RELATIONSHIPS	Talks back to grown-ups	1	2	3	4	5	49
	Disobeys parents	1	2	3	4	5	50
	Can't be trusted	1	2	3	4	5	51
	Has a 'chip on the shoulder	1	2	3	4	5	52
	Doesn't trust other people	1	2	3	4	5	53
EMOTIONAL PROBLEMS	Is sad or unhappy much of the time	1	2	3	4	5	55
	Cries a lot	1	2	3	4	5	56
	Has temper tantrums	1	2	3	4	5	57
	Mood changes quickly or without reason	1	2	3	4	5	58
	Has threatened or attempted suicide	1	2	3	4	5	60
	Hurts self on purpose	1	2	3	4	5	61
	Acts younger than real age	1	2	3	4	5	62
	Can't sit still	1	2	3	4	5	63
OTHER PROBLEMS	Acts without thinking	1	2	3	4	5	64
	Wants things to be perfect	1	2	3	4	5	65
	Says or does strange or peculiar things	1	2	3	4	5	66
	Is often confused or in a daze	1	2	3	4	5	67
	Daydreams a lot	1	2	3	4	5	68
	Doesn't finish things (short attention span)	1	2	3	4	5	69

Now, please describe in your own words why you want your child to be evaluated at this time:

_____

_____

_____

_____

_____

Any other information which you feel is important:

_____

_____

_____

_____   _____
Signature of Person Completing Form   Relation to Child

FOR ADMINISTRATIVE USE ONLY. PLEASE DO NOT WRITE IN THIS SPACE.

Information Requested: ☐ School ☐ Medical ☐ Social Agency

Date of Intake Review

Case referred to:
☐ Neurology ☐ Psychology ☐ Social Service

Case was: ☐ Deferred ☐ Rejected

OPD APPOINTMENT

Date Scheduled	Time Scheduled	Doctor

☐ Appointment Mailed ☐ Appointment Phoned ☐ Appointment Confirmed ☐ Appointment Cancelled

If cancelled, reason for cancellation, and other information:

LAFAYETTE CLINIC
DIVISION OF CHILD AND ADOLESCENT PSYCHIATRY

951 E. Lafayette

Detroit, Michigan 48207

SEQUENCE NO.

C	2	0	1				
1			4		6		9

TEACHER RATING AND SCHOOL INFORMATION

FORM MAILED _____ / _____ / 19 _____

TO:
PRINCIPAL OF _____

(NAME OF SCHOOL)

NUMBER AND STREET NAME		CITY		STATE	ZIP CODE

CHILD'S NAME	First	Middle	Last	SEX	BIRTHDATE
11				☐ M ☐ F	_____ / _____ / 19 _____
			30	32	34 43

The above named child or adolescent has been referred to the Division of Child and Adolescent Psychiatry at Lafayette Clinic. To help us in our evaluation of this student, would you please see that this questionnaire is completed by the staff members who are most familiar with this child. In addition, it is **extremely** important that all psychological, psychiatric and social work information be forwarded to our department. Release of information forms have already been signed and are enclosed.

Please return this complete questionnaire in the envelope provided. Your cooperation is greatly appreciated.

Thank you,

Intake Secretary
Telephone

Please respond to each item: (To be completed by Principal or Social Worker)

☐ ☐   1. The school has information regarding a psychological assessment of this child. These results will be forwarded to
YES NO   Lafayette Clinic.

☐ ☐   2. The school has information regarding social work contacts and a summary will be forwarded to Lafayette Clinic.
YES NO

☐ ☐   3. Psychiatric or other evaluation material are available and will be forwarded to Lafayette Clinic.
YES NO

_____
PRINCIPAL'S SIGNATURE

_____
DATE

TELEPHONE NO.   EXTENTION

DMH-2-771-P

EVALUATION OF BEHAVIOR PROBLEMS: (To be completed by the teacher(s) and other school staff who have had the most contact with this student). Please read each statement carefully and decide if you have observed that behavior items in the child's response pattern during the last two month period (or during the last two months of school, if this form is completed during summer vacation). If you have observed the behavior described in the statement during this period, place an 'X' in the "YES" column, if not, place an 'X' in the "NO" column.

C	2	0	2
1			4

YES	NO	COL	Statement
		11	Complains about others' unfairness and/or discrimination towards him.
		12	Is listless and continually tired.
		13	Does not conform to limits on his own without control from others.
		14	Becomes hysterical, upset or angry when things do not go his way.
		15	Comments that no one understands him.
		16	Perfectionistic: meticulous about having everything exactly right.
		17	Will destroy or take apart something he has made rather than show it or ask to have it displayed.
		18	Other children act as if he were taboo or tainted.
		19	Has difficulty concentrating for any length of time.
		20	Is overactive, restless, and/or continually shifting body positions.
		21	Apologizes repeatedly for himself and/or his behavior.

YES	NO	COL	Statement
		35	Comments that nobody likes him.
		36	Repeats one idea, thought, or activity over and over.
		37	Has temper tantrums.
		38	Refers to himself as dumb, stupid, or incapable.
		39	Does not engage in group activities.
		40	When teased or irritated by other children, takes out his frustration(s) on another inappropriate person or thing.
		41	Has rapid mood shifts: depressed one moment, manic the next.
		42	Does not obey until threatened with punishment.
		43	Complains of nightmares, bad dreams.
		44	Expresses concern about being lonely, unhappy.
		45	Openly strikes back with angry behavior to teasing of other children.

46. Expresses concern about something terrible or horrible happening to him.
47. Has no friends.
48. Must have approval for tasks attempted or completed.
49. Displays physical aggression towards objects or persons.
50. Is hypercritical of himself.
51. Does not complete tasks attempted.
52. Doesn't protest when others hurt, tease, or criticize him.
53. Shuns or avoids heterosexual activities.
54. Steals things from other children.
55. Does not initiate relationships with other children.
56. Reacts with defiance to instructions or commands.
57. Weeps or cries without provocation.
58. Stutters, stammers, or blocks on saying words.
59. Easily distracted away from the task at hand by ordinary classroom stimuli, i.e., minor movements of others, noises, etc.
60. Frequently stares blankly into space and is unaware of his surroundings when doing so.

22. Distorts the truth by making statements contrary to fact.
23. Underachieving: performs below his demonstrated ability level.
24. Disturbs other children: teasing, provoking fights, interrupting others.
25. Tries to avoid calling attention to himself.
26. Makes distrustful or suspicious remarks about actions of others toward him.
27. Reacts to stressful situations or changes in routine with general body aches, head or stomach aches, nausea.
28. Argues and must have the last word in verbal exchanges.
29. Approaches new tasks and situations with an "I can't do it" response.
30. Has nervous tics: muscle-twitching, eye-blinking, nail-biting, hand-wringing.
31. Habitually rejects the school experience through actions or comments.
32. Has enuresis. (Wets bed.)
33. Utters nonsense syllables and/or babbles to himself.
34. Continually seeks attention.

Punch In Column
11 – 12

C	2	0	3
1			4

Place an 'X' to indicate this student's current grade placement
(last completed grade, if during summer):

REGULAR CLASSES:

K	1	2	3	4	5	6	7	8	9	10	11	12

OR

SPECIAL EDUCATION: [13] Mentally impaired   [14] Learning disabled   [15] Emotionally impaired

Please compare this child's current achievement with other children of the same **age** and place an 'X' to indicate the appropriate achievement level in each area:

ACHIEVEMENT LEVEL	1 or more years above	Average	1-2 years below	*2 or more years below	Do not know	COLUMNS
English/Language skills	1	2	3	4	5	17
Phonic skills	1	2	3	4	5	18
Reading Comprehension	1	2	3	4	5	19
Spelling	1	2	3	4	5	20
Handwriting	1	2	3	4	5	21
Mathematics	1	2	3	4	5	22
Physical Education	1	2	3	4	5	23
Verbal Expression	1	2	3	4	5	24

If any area of this child's achievement is below age expectation, please indicate the reasons you feel form the basis for this difficulty. (mark all items that apply):

'X'	COL		'X'	COL
Below average intelligence	26	Has problems with vision		39
Doesn't pay attention in class	27	Has difficulty understanding instructions		40
Frequent daydreaming	28	Poor gross motor coordination (running, etc.)		41
Poor class attendance	29	Poor fine motor coordination (drawing, etc.)		42
Doesn't complete homework	30	Bored/not interested		43

Doesn't complete class assignments	31	Lacks basic skills from previous classes	44
Gives up easily/expects failure	32	Bilingual	45
Distractible/limited concentration	33	Hungry/poor nutrition	46
Restless/fidgety	34	Emotional problems	47
Listless/constantly tired	35	Family uninterested in child's education	48
Poor study skills	36	Talkative	49
Impulsively reacts (behaves) without thinking	37	Speech problems (articulation/phonation)	50
Has problems with hearing	38		

At this point, what would be your recommendation for the most appropriate (ideal) class placement?

	'X'	COL.
Remain at present grade placement		52
Remain at present grade placement, but needs special attention/remedial tutoring		53
Remain at present grade placement, but repeat grade next year		54
Transfer to special education: emotionally impaired		55
Transfer to special education: learning disabled		56
Transfer to special education: mentally impaired		57
Transfer to vocational training program		58
Demote to earlier grade		59
Promote to a higher grade		60
Re-evaluate for possible return to regular classroom (if now in special education)		61

Has this child repeated a regular grade? (63)

☐ Yes ☐ No

If "YES," indicate the number of times that grade(s) has been repeated.

K	1	2	3	4	5	6	7	8	9	10	11	12
65	66	67	68	69	70	71	72	73	74	75	76	77

Considering your total teaching experience with children of this age, how much of a problem is the child at this time?

None	Mild	Moderate	Severe	Column
1	2	3	4	79

SCHOOLS ATTENDED	DATE OF ADMISSION	DAYS ABSENT	DATE OF LEAVING	REASON FOR LEAVING

(Please feel free to continue your comments on additional paper.)

Specific Problem Behaviors: (Briefly summarize this child's specific behavior problems as **you** see them in the classroom)

_____

_____

_____

Health or Physical Problems if any: (i.e., wears glasses, falls asleep in class, poor grooming, etc.)

_____

_____

Student's Reaction to Success and Failure:

_____

_____

_____

Family Attitude Toward School and the Student:

_____

_____

_____

What are your personal reactions to this student?

_____

_____

_____

_____   _____
Signature (Primary person filling out report)   Title   Date

LAFAYETTE CLINIC
DIVISION OF CHILD AND ADOLESCENT PSYCHIATRY
951 E. LAFAYETTE
DETROIT, MICHIGAN 48207

DESCRIPTION OF CURRENT PROBLEM BEHAVIORS

C	3	0	1
1		4	

SEQUENCE NO.

6		9

CHILD'S NAME	First	Middle	Last	SEX	BIRTHDATE	PATIENT NO.
11				30	32	34	43 44	48

SEX: ☐ M ☐ F

BIRTHDATE: __ / __ / 19 __

RACE (49)
1 White
2 Black
3 Oriental
4 Latino
5 Other

STATUS (50)
1 Inpatient
2 Outpatient
3 Research

REFERRAL
SOURCE (51)
1 Parent
2 School
3 Mental Hlth. Agency
4 Private Psychiatrist
5 Court
6 Family Physician

RATER _____

DATE OF INTERVIEW __ / __ / 19 __

52   69 70   79

DIRECTIONS: This form should be completed immediately following an interview with a patient and their family. Most items allow three possible responses: "Y" - item is *clearly* supported by interview data or history which reflects the *past six months* ~~inference can be avoided. "N", not supported by history or evaluation. "?", unsure, or relevant data unavailable.~~

C	3	0	2
1			4

SELF CONCEPT

	Y	N	?	COL.
Overly critical of self				11
Usually expects failure				12
Expects rejection from others				13

AFFECT

	Y	N	?	COL.
Unrealistic fears				15
Rapid mood shifts (sad or angry one day, happy the next)				16
Self-destructive behavior (wrist-slashing, head-banging, etc.)				17
Expresses suicidal thoughts or ideations				18
Verbally hostile or argumentative				19
Destructive of objects				20
Expresses feelings of sadness or unhappiness				21
Frequent crying				22
Separation anxiety				23
Easily upset or irritable				24
Expresses feelings of anxiety, tension, nervousness or restlessness				25
Manifests 'nervous habits' (thumb sucking, nail biting, scratching, pulling and twisting hair, or grimacing)				26
Worries a great deal				27
Inappropriate affect				28

COGNITIVE FUNCTIONING

	Y	N	?	COL.
Displays receptive aphasic symptoms (doesn't seem to comprehend spoken language well)				29
Displays expressive aphasic symtoms (unable to find words to express ideas; uses general or related word rather than specific word desired)				30
Displays an associative (thought) disorder				31

Functions at below average intellectual level. (if YES, mark only one)

□ Mild (32)   □ Moderate (33)   □ Severe (34)

DMH-2-722-P

	C	3	0	2
1				4

	Y	N	?	COL.
Poor judgment/needs much supervision				35
Frequently frustrated				36
Impulsive behavior				37
Disorganized (bizarre) behavior				38
Poor recent or remote memory				39
Mute/primitive verbal skills				40
Hallucinations				41
Delusions of persecution/paranoia				42
Exaggerated sense of self-importance/grandiosity				43
Concrete thinking beyond age expectation				44
Complains of poor concentration/is easily distracted				45
Frequently unresponsive to surroundings				46
Lack of interest in environment				47
Obsessive thought pattern				48
Seems bright in many ways, but still achieves poorly in school				49

	C	3	0	3
1				4

INTERPERSONAL RELATIONS

	Y	N	?	COL.
Often a poor sport and poor loser				11
Has few or no friends				12
Seeks excessive approval				13
Pseudomature behavior				14
Overly conforming/passive follower				15
Overly controlling/bossy				16
Described as being selfish				17
Excessive shyness				18

No.	Item			
19	Isolative (usually plays alone, stays in room, etc.)			
20	Excessive daydreaming			
21	Distrustful or suspicious of others			
22	Decreased verbal communicaton/seldom talks			
23	Disobedient to parents			
24	Running away from home			
25	Resistant to change in the environment			
26	Temper tantrums			
27	Disobediance to teachers or breaks school rules			
28	History of physical fights with peers			
29	Complains of peer hostility and discrimination			
30	Friends are mainly younger than child			
31	Friends are mainly older than child			
32	Displays irresponsible behavior			
33	Blames others for his/her problems			
34	Frequent fights with siblings			
35	Teases peers			
36	Teased by peers			
37	Firesetting			
38	Lying			
39	Stealing			
40	Truancy			
41	Vandalism			
42	Involved with the police			
43	Excessive masturbation			
44	Precocious sexual behavior or promiscuity			
45	Gender identification disturbance (overly feminine male, or overly masculine female)			

C	3	0	4
1			4

PHYSICAL DEVELOPMENT AND HEALTH

	Y	N	?	COL.
Sleep disturbance: Has nightmares/bad dreams				11
Awakens early				12
Has difficulty getting to sleep				13
Excessive sleeping				14
Encopresis: continuing				15
Encopresis: regressive				16
Nocturnal enuresis: continuing				17
Nocturnal enuresis: regressive				18
Diurnal enuresis: continuing				19
Diurnal enuresis: regressive				20
Intentional enuresis: continuing				21
Intentional enuresis: regressive				22
Speech disturbance: articulation				23
phonation				24
rhythm				25
immature				26
stuttering or stammering				27
echolalia				28
Somatic response to stress (e.g., stomachaches)				29
Inappropiate somatic concern (hypochondriasis)				30
Headaches				31
Chronic pain				32
Sensory deficit in hearing				33
Sensory deficit in vision				34
Listless and continually tired				35
Retarded physical growth				36

		COL.
Decreased appetite		37
Overeating		38
Overactive or agitated		39
Compulsive or ritualistic behavior		40
Perfectionistic or meticulous behavior		41
Abnormal motor behavior (spinning, hand flapping, gesturing, etc.)		42
Gross motor ataxia (clumsiness): mild		43
moderate/severe		44
Fine motor ataxia (clumsiness): mild		45
moderate/severe		46
Previous psychiatric hospitalization		47
Previous outpatient psychotherapy		48
Previous psychotropic medication: stimulants		49
minor tranquilizer		50
major tranquilizer		51
antidepressants		52
anticonvulsants		53

OTHER

	Y	N	?	COL.
School refusal				54
Expresses a dislike for school				55
Achievement in school at least one year below chronological age grade placement(underachievement)				56
History of problematic substance (drug) abuse				57
History of problematic alcohol abuse				58
Untidy and careless in self-appearance				59
Overt refusal to answer interview questions (uncooperative)				60
Defensive in interview (denies obvious negative affect or behavior)				61

142

Appendix A

C	3	0	5
1			4

FAMILY RELATIONS

	Y	N	?	COL.
Child expresses strong dislike of a member of their family				11
Child was born out of wedlock				12
Biological parents are currently divorced or separated				13
Parents present a history of marital discord				14

PARENT DESCRIPTION

	MOTHER				FATHER			
	Y	N	?	COL.	Y	N	?	COL.
Defensive (about self) in interview				15				26
Minimizes child's problems				16				27
Emotionally disturbed (in need of individual treatment)				17				28
Overly concerned or overly protective				18				29
Rejecting or overly critical of child				19				30
Strict disciplinarian				20				31
Uses excessive physical punishment				21				32
Inconsistent in setting limits				22				33
Overly permissive, difficulty in setting limits				23				34
Alcoholic or other substance abuser				24				35
Familial history of mental illness or epilepsy				25				36

DIAGNOSIS

Primary DSM II Dx: _____

Code: [ ][ ][ ][ ][ ][ ]
37   42

Primary GAP Dx: _____

Code: [ ][ ]
44 45

(see code sheet)

IDEAL RECOMMENDATIONS (mark all that apply)	'X'	COL.
No intervention necessary		47
Refer for psychiatric hospitalization		48
Refer for outpatient individual therapy		49
Refer for parent counseling		50
Refer for family therapy		51
Chemotherapy indicated for patient: (1) stimulants		52
(2) minor tranquilizers		53
(3) major tranquilizers		54
(4) anti-depressants		55
(5) anti-convulsants		56
This chemotherapy represents: (mark only one) (1) a new treatment approach; patient currently drug-free		57
(2) a change from current chemotherapy		58
(3) continuation on current chemotherapy		59
Prognosis for remediation of current problems: (mark only one) (1) excellent		60
(2) good		61
(3) guarded		62
(4) poor		63
(5) can't tell		64
Specific recommendations to school		65
Specific recommendations to court, social agency, etc.		66

Appendix B
Criterion Frequency (%) by PIC Scale T-Score Range
I: Replicated Correlates Selected for the Total Study Sample

L SCALE CORRELATES	BR	30-39 n=182	40-49 n=164	50-59 n=49	≧ 60 n=36
Pre-Appointment Information					
Fights with other children	49	65	45	33	17
Lies	62	77	59	43	29
Breaks things	40	48	41	29	11
Poor loser	53	67	50	33	28
Demands too much attention	55	67	49	47	34
Disobeys parents	66	81	66	37	29
Can't be trusted	52	69	48	29	20
Has temper tantrums	57	69	50	51	36
Acts without thinking	72	81	71	63	40
Hangs around with a "bad crowd"	38	51	33	17	15
Often skips school	41	55	37	17	14
Runs away from home	32	40	30	30	5
Teacher Rating and School Information					
None					
Description of Current Problem Behaviors					
Poor judgment/needs much supervision	53	61	54	40	25
Complains of poor concentration/is easily distracted	52	58	55	40	28
Disobedient to parents	62	79	57	37	31
Runs away from home	27	36	25	12	8
Lying	48	69	38	23	30

F SCALE CORRELATES

	BR	30-59 n=60	60-69 n=69	70-79 n=81	80-89 n=89	90-99 n=45	100-109 n=42	≥110 n=45
Pre-Appointment Information								
Refuses to go to bed	30	14	20	25	30	29	41	60
Trouble falling asleep	32	12	22	34	34	31	36	67
Has few or no friends	49	27	39	55	46	62	57	73
Has sex play with other children	14	5	3	10	18	27	19	20
Runs away from home	21	7	13	27	21	29	29	29
Breaks things	40	22	32	36	39	40	57	67
Disobeys parents	66	48	48	72	71	76	86	71
Can't be trusted	52	31	39	49	53	62	73	73
Has temper tantrums	57	47	45	49	55	73	71	76
Says or does strange or peculiar things	42	17	23	42	47	58	60	64
Is often confused or in a daze	40	31	26	30	46	40	52	60
Teacher Rating and School Information								
None								
Description of Current Problem Behaviors								
Destructive of objects	38	27	27	49	37	34	38	58
Temper tantrums	43	37	31	34	47	52	50	62
Displays irresponsible behavior	47	29	45	42	48	53	57	62
Mother overly permissive in setting limits	41	27	44	39	30	50	63	58
Refer for psychiatric hospitalization	33	18	17	36	36	42	52	42

DEF SCALE CORRELATES

	BR	0-19 n=23	20-29 n=38	30-39 n=88	40-49 n=105	50-59 n=117	60-69 n=41	≥70 n=19
Pre-Appointment Information								
Poor loser	53	83	54	58	52	53	37	37
Teacher Rating and School Information								
None								
Description of Current Problem Behaviors								
None								

ADJ SCALE CORRELATES	BR	40-59 n=43	60-69 n=49	70-79 n=75	80-89 n=84	90-99 n=89	100-109 n=55	≥ 110 n=36
Pre-Appointment Information								
Slow to walk by self	11	5	4	8	11	8	20	33
Slow to toilet train	10	2	6	4	11	10	20	22
Clumsy or accident prone	37	17	29	28	38	40	53	56
Has problems learning in school	61	37	47	47	64	72	73	89
Has few or no friends	49	12	22	44	51	61	62	89
Plays alone most of the time	44	14	22	40	50	42	62	81
Fights with other children	49	33	39	32	54	49	73	75
Has sex play with other children	14	5	2	9	14	15	20	36
Steals	35	14	22	28	30	39	56	64
Breaks things	40	19	22	25	45	41	55	81
Talks back to grown-ups	58	31	51	43	60	64	86	69
Can't be trusted	52	21	37	41	45	60	78	89
Disobeys parents	66	29	55	49	69	78	91	83
Has temper tantrums	57	35	49	41	60	64	80	69
Hurts self on purpose	14	7	4	12	13	17	18	31
Acts without thinking	72	43	63	71	73	71	90	92
Is often confused or in a daze	40	14	33	32	39	48	44	69
Doesn't finish things (short attention span)	71	42	55	60	68	76	86	97

...conform to limits or rules/ her own without control from others	63	37	55	55	71	63	72	82
Distorts the truth by making statements contrary to fact	46	20	34	40	55	53	60	49
Habitually rejects the school experience through actions or comments	40	25	32	39	39	45	47	50
Doesn't obey until threatened with punishment	41	14	34	35	49	50	40	58
Openly strikes back with angry behavior to teasing of other children	42	29	25	30	41	51	60	55
Displays physical aggression towards objects or persons	42	29	25	32	49	47	51	63
Reacts with defiance to instructions or commands	38	25	30	31	38	43	49	52
Teacher rating of magnitude of problem	75	55	64	64	84	85	80	87
Description of Current Problem Behaviors								
Overly critical of self	24	25	13	21	23	25	27	38
Destructive of objects	38	28	20	28	35	44	50	67
Poor judgment/needs much supervision	53	27	38	51	57	61	67	59
Described as being selfish	24	5	15	24	16	33	36	42
Disobedient to parents	62	36	38	63	60	72	80	76
Temper tantrums	43	28	26	36	38	52	63	65
Disobediance to teachers or breaks school rules	50	30	39	41	53	54	61	74
Lying	48	27	31	39	52	54	70	63
Stealing	32	12	24	26	35	33	54	39

ACH SCALE CORRELATES	BR	20-49 n=62	50-59 n=119	60-69 n=105	70-79 n=90	≥80 n=55
Pre-Appointment Information						
Slow to first walk by self	11	3	8	7	11	38
Doesn't speak well	18	7	13	15	22	43
Has problems learning in school	61	23	46	67	84	89
Breaks things	40	18	28	41	59	57
Acts younger than real age	45	20	29	53	57	76
Is often confused or in a daze	40	25	29	42	48	61
Doesn't finish things (short attention span)	71	45	65	76	81	83
Teacher Rating and School Information						
Has difficulty concentrating for any length of time	69	45	66	70	77	84
Approaches new tasks and situations with an "I can't do it" response	36	26	31	28	45	60
Below average achievement in:						
• English/language skills	57	23	43	60	75	88
• Phonic skills	51	25	27	51	76	88
• Reading comprehension	56	13	41	59	75	95
• Spelling	54	20	35	55	73	93
• Handwriting	40	11	28	39	57	78
• Mathematics	58	22	48	62	73	91
• Verbal expression	33	10	17	37	46	66
Below average intelligence	10	2	4	10	12	33
Doesn't pay attention in class	40	21	31	40	56	58
Frequent daydreaming	28	11	23	32	32	40
Doesn't complete class assignments	46	34	34	54	53	58
Gives up easily/expects failure	27	15	15	30	33	49
Has difficulty understanding instructions	20	8	13	17	32	35
Speech problems (articulation/phonation)	7	2	3	8	10	16
Transfer to special education:						

	8	2	4	9	9	20
Displays receptive aphasic symptoms (doesn't seem to comprehend spoken language well)	8	2	4	9	9	20
Displays expressive aphasic symptoms (unable to find words to express ideas; uses general or related word rather than specific word desired)	10	3	3	8	15	26
Functions at below average intelligence level:						
• Mild	27	10	20	26	40	40
• Moderate/Severe	15	2	8	14	20	36
Poor judgment/needs much supervision	53	38	42	60	60	74
Mute/primitive verbal skills	13	7	7	13	17	29
Concrete thinking beyond age expectation	22	5	14	25	27	45
Decreased verbal communication/seldom talks	20	3	19	20	24	34
Speech disturbance:						
• Articulation	16	7	9	20	19	32
• Phonation	8	2	3	5	10	26
• Immature	13	2	8	11	20	33
Gross motor ataxia (clumsiness):						
Mild	16	5	8	18	26	30
Fine motor ataxia (clumsiness):						
Mild	22	13	11	19	33	43
Previous psychotropic medication:						
Stimulants	21	7	15	20	33	33
Achievement in school at least one year below chronological age grade placement (underachievement)	59	23	48	60	75	96
Untidy and careless in self-appearance	12	8	6	15	8	34
Specific recommendations to school	31	18	22	32	41	46
Poor prognosis for remediation of current problems	51	29	50	52	53	76

IS SCALE CORRELATES	BR	0-39 n=46	40-49 n=87	50-59 n=80	60-69 n=73	70-79 n=58	80-89 n=37	90-109 n=28	≥110 n=22
Pre-Appointment Information									
Slow to first dress self	8	4	3	6	8	7	11	18	27
Slow to speak first real sentences	20	13	10	20	18	21	22	32	55
Doesn't speak well	18	4	6	18	21	25	32	25	46
Has problems learning in school	61	41	46	53	73	67	76	89	82
Acts younger than real age	45	26	28	46	42	47	70	71	82
Teacher Rating and School Information									
Other children act as if he/she were taboo or tainted	25	23	16	16	19	29	28	60	48
Repeats one idea, thought, or activity over and over	19	10	10	11	18	21	22	44	57
Below average achievement in:									
• English/language skills	57	35	36	46	63	69	77	78	89
• Phonic skills	51	22	27	43	53	64	71	82	85
• Reading comprehension	56	29	30	42	64	67	74	96	95
• Spelling	54	24	33	54	52	55	71	96	90
• Handwriting	40	23	22	30	37	43	65	91	71
• Mathematics	58	30	42	47	64	68	63	100	95
• Verbal expression	33	21	20	24	40	28	43	58	74
Below average intelligence	10	9	7	4	8	9	11	36	32
Gives up easily/expects failure	27	20	20	21	32	26	32	43	46
Has problems with vision	14	4	9	14	10	21	16	32	23
Lacks basic skills from previous classes	25	20	10	10	33	40	35	46	32
Transfer to special education:									
• Learning disabled	9		2	0	8	16	8	25	18

Displays receptive aphasic symptoms (doesn't seem to comprehend spoken language well)	8	4	2	5	4	11	18	11	35
Functions at below average intellectual level:									
• Mild	27	13	15	26	30	40	33	41	32
• Moderate/Severe	15	11	5	4	11	24	22	33	55
• Total	42	24	20	30	41	64	55	74	87
Decreased verbal communication/ seldom talks	20	21	16	13	18	21	29	25	43
Friends are mainly younger than child	14	7	3	11	13	19	21	41	33
Speech disturbance:									
• Articulation	16	2	6	21	12	19	19	33	46
• Immature	13	0	6	12	14	16	19	29	43
• Echolalia	2	0	0	1	1	0	6	7	18
Gross motor ataxia (clumsiness):									
• Mild	16	9	5	21	14	14	27	41	29
• Moderate/Severe	3	2	0	0	1	2	5	7	19
Fine motor ataxia (clumsiness):									
• Mild	22	9	8	19	19	32	31	59	36
Previous psychotropic medication: Stimulants	21	12	15	15	25	16	34	41	40
Achievement in school at least one year below chronological age grade placement (underachievement)	59	37	50	44	57	67	77	92	100
Untidy and careless in self-appearance	12	9	11	10	7	14	14	37	14

DVL SCALE CORRELATES	BR	20-49 n=85	50-59 n=124	60-69 n=105	70-79 n=74	≥80 n=43
Pre-Appointment Information						
Slow to first stand alone	5	4	2	1	10	21
Slow to walk by self	11	7	7	8	12	42
Slow to speak first real words	24	15	25	22	20	49
Doesn't speak well	18	8	15	16	26	40
Has problems learning in school	61	22	52	76	81	93
Acts younger than real age	45	23	33	51	65	77
Doesn't finish things (short attention span)	71	45	71	74	81	93
Teacher Rating and School Information						
Approaches new tasks and situations with an "I can't do it" response	36	26	27	40	46	58
Doesn't complete tasks attempted	64	49	60	69	73	74
Easily distracted away from the task at hand by ordinary classroom stimuli	64	49	62	68	65	82
Below average achievement in:						
• English/language skills	57	27	53	56	76	94
• Phonic skills	51	18	39	57	77	90
• Reading comprehension	56	16	53	56	82	97
• Spelling	54	19	43	59	80	93
• Handwriting	40	15	31	42	58	89
• Mathematics	58	32	47	60	86	94
• Physical education	24	6	15	28	36	56
• Verbal expression	33	5	25	35	57	71
Below average intelligence	10	1	9	8	15	33
Doesn't pay attention in class	40	22	35	46	49	65
Doesn't complete class assignments	46	26	46	51	55	56
Gives up easily/expects failure	27	14	21	30	34	49
Poor study skills	35	18	33	44	39	44
Has difficulty understanding instructions	20	5	19	15	31	47
Lacks basic skills from previous classes	25	9	16	32	32	47

...to special education:						
• Emotionally impaired	13	6	7	16	16	30
• Learning disabled	9	1	8	10	11	26
• Mentally impaired (mentally retarded)	3	0	1	0	5	14
Teacher rating of magnitude of problem	75	60	75	78	80	89
Description of Current Problem Behaviors						
Displays receptive aphasic symptoms (doesn't seem to comprehend spoken language well)	8	1	7	5	15	21
Displays expressive aphasic symptoms (unable to find words to express ideas; uses general or related word rather than specific word desired)	10	2	8	4	16	33
Poor judgment/needs much supervision	53	42	52	49	59	79
Concrete thinking beyond age expectation	22	5	15	20	34	59
Decreased verbal communication/seldom talks	20	11	16	18	30	38
Speech disturbance:						
• Articulation	16	5	17	11	25	36
• Phonation	8	2	5	4	12	29
• Immature	13	0	9	8	29	41
Gross motor ataxia (clumsiness): Mild	16	7	11	17	25	36
Fine motor ataxia (clumsiness): Mild	22	16	13	19	32	50
Previous psychotropic medication: Stimulants	21	12	13	26	33	29
Achievement in school at least one year below chronological age grade placement (underachievement)	59	25	50	70	77	97
Untidy and careless in self-appearance	12	5	11	14	18	19
Poor prognosis for remediation of current problems	51	35	55	51	61	65
Specific recommendations to school	31	12	28	38	37	49

SOM SCALE CORRELATES	BR	30-49 n=59	50-59 n=86	60-69 n=114	70-79 n=81	80-89 n=63	≥90 n=28
Pre-Appointment Information							
Tired most of the time	28	14	20	21	34	46	61
Has aches and pains	38	20	28	29	50	54	68
Fakes being sick	27	14	15	23	41	43	36
Teacher Rating and School Information							
None							
Description of Current Problem Behaviors							
Chronic pain	5	0	5	1	6	13	18

D SCALE CORRELATES	BR	30-49 n=36	50-59 n=62	60-69 n=99	70-79 n=96	80-89 n=81	≥90 n=57
Pre-Appointment Information							
Doesn't eat right	27	14	13	21	23	40	46
Refuses to go to bed	30	23	15	22	32	40	46
Trouble falling asleep	32	14	21	17	41	41	56
Has aches and pains	38	8	23	32	45	43	61
Is afraid to go to school	18	6	5	15	18	24	39
Has few or no friends	49	11	23	39	53	78	74
Plays alone most of the time	44	17	19	30	42	68	81
Afraid of many things	27	0	16	19	27	38	51
Doesn't trust other people	31	11	15	16	39	51	47
Is sad or unhappy much of the time	53	3	28	38	63	77	84
Cries a lot	37	8	19	27	47	44	61
Mood changes quickly or without reason	66	37	61	54	73	75	83
Wants things to be perfect	34	19	19	25	42	44	48
Teacher Rating and School Information							
None							
Description of Current Problem Behaviors							
Overly critical of self	24	11	25	16	20	31	45
Excessive shyness	24	11	10	21	20	35	38
Isolative (usually plays alone, stays in room, etc.)	40	15	27	28	45	57	59
Mother overly permissive, difficulty in setting limits	41	23	40	33	39	51	60

FAM SCALE CORRELATES	BR	30-49 n=71	50-59 n=124	60-69 n=121	70-79 n=84	≥ 80 n=31
Pre-Appointment Information						
None						
Teacher Rating and School Information						
None						
Description of Current Problem Behaviors						
Biological parents are currently divorced or separated	59	33	55	67	71	68
Parents present a history or marital discord	70	41	59	75	93	87
Mother emotionally disturbed (in need of individual treatment)	43	16	36	45	64	57
Mother inconsistent in setting limits	59	30	53	65	69	82
Mother alcoholic or other substance abuser	8	2	5	7	14	26
Father rejecting or overly critical of child	31	19	25	36	27	73
Father alcoholic or other substance abuser	36	26	31	30	50	85

DLQ SCALE CORRELATES	BR	30-59 n=51	60-69 n=61	70-79 n=87	80-89 n=73	90-99 n=62	100-109 n=33	110-119 n=32	≥120 n=32
Pre-Appointment Information									
Refuses to go to bed	30	18	26	23	33	36	33	42	38
Won't obey school rules	57	22	38	45	60	77	73	84	91
Often skips school	25	0	7	10	15	32	39	71	88
Picks on other children	42	24	30	37	52	57	39	48	53
Fights with other children	49	28	39	39	60	65	61	58	56
Has sex play with other children	14	2	7	9	14	15	24	26	34
Hangs around with a "bad crowd"	27	6	7	16	19	32	55	58	81
Uses drugs	12	0	7	6	7	11	18	32	53
Runs away from home	21	0	8	12	19	26	24	61	56
Lies	62	44	36	48	73	71	79	90	91
Steals	35	12	5	23	41	52	52	74	63
Sets fires	14	4	13	9	21	15	18	19	16
Breaks things	40	14	25	41	51	50	42	55	44
Talks back to grown-ups	58	14	43	49	71	69	67	84	91
Disobeys parents	66	18	39	64	77	86	82	97	88
Can't be trusted	52	18	23	43	62	63	79	84	87
Has a "chip on the shoulder"	49	16	36	37	51	58	70	87	75
Has temper tantrums	57	22	43	52	71	71	61	74	75
Teacher Rating and School Information									
Complains about others' unfairness and/or discrimination toward him/her	50	24	35	50	62	56	63	52	61
Doesn't conform to limits on his/her own without control from others	63	29	65	59	68	72	67	67	91
Distorts the truth by making statements contrary to fact	46	22	33	40	55	60	53	59	64
Argues and must have the last word in verbal exchanges	37	16	35	30	45	48	50	37	52
Habitually rejects the school experience through actions or comments	40	16	26	40	42	50	47	56	67

DLQ SCALE CORRELATES CONTINUED

	BR	30-59 n=51	60-69 n=61	70-79 n=87	80-89 n=73	90-99 n=62	100-109 n=33	110-119 n=32	≥120 n=32
Teacher Rating and School Information (contd.)									
Doesn't obey until threatened with punishment	41	18	35	39	50	46	47	52	59
Openly strikes back with angry behavior to teasing of other children	42	20	33	37	53	58	47	41	46
Displays physical aggression toward objects or persons	42	16	37	39	53	58	43	48	48
Doesn't complete tasks attempted	64	33	60	66	70	72	57	70	91
Steals things from other children	14	4	6	5	22	16	23	23	29
Reacts with defiance to instructions or commands	38	11	31	34	42	44	60	41	68
Poor class attendance	24	4	21	21	27	19	24	50	47
Bored/not interested	30	18	20	22	32	27	52	50	47
Transfer to special education: Emotionally impaired	13	8	5	12	11	16	15	31	16
Description of Current Problem Behaviors									
Verbally hostile or argumentative	48	22	39	42	48	57	56	75	63
Impulsive behavior	68	40	57	61	72	76	72	84	100
Described as being selfish	24	10	14	17	34	25	39	38	32
Disobedient to parents	62	26	41	62	75	66	72	90	88
Temper tantrums	43	18	42	40	38	44	63	64	69
Disobedient to teachers or breaks school rules	50	28	38	46	49	57	57	63	81
Friends are mainly older than child	17	5	11	9	21	15	36	22	42
Displays irresponsible behavior	47	22	30	37	61	43	69	57	92
Blames others for his/her problems	39	17	26	37	46	51	54	41	48
Lying	48	23	30	44	60	49	62	75	74
Stealing	32	9	14	23	40	42	37	62	63
Truancy	26	5	13	16	15	35	27	63	82
Involved with the police	17	0	4	6	10	21	19	58	63
Expresses a dislike for school	39	28	28	28	30	48	55	63	70

WDL SCALE CORRELATES	BR	30-49 n=59	50-59 n=118	60-69 n=115	70-79 n=55	80-89 n=56	≥90 n=27
Mother emotionally disturbed (in need of individual treatment)	43	25	31	59	58	50	62
Mother inconsistent in setting limits	59	27	45	59	82	89	67
Father inconsistent in setting limits	46	14	33	45	89	56	64
Refer for psychiatric hospitalization	33	20	21	26	39	53	72
Poor prognosis for remediation of current problems	51	23	42	50	61	77	68
Pre-Appointment Information							
Is afraid to go to school	18	7	13	17	24	30	37
Plays alone most of the time	44	19	28	46	55	75	74
Very shy	26	16	11	20	27	50	85
Teacher Rating and School Information							
Doesn't engage in group activities	37	21	27	40	51	48	58
Description of Current Problem Behaviors							
Excessive shyness	24	14	13	25	28	33	58
Isolative (usually plays alone, stays in room, etc.)	40	21	27	39	57	59	72

ANX SCALE CORRELATES	BR	30-49 n=49	50-59 n=86	60-69 n=138	70-79 n=87	80-89 n=50	≥90 n=20
Pre-Appointment Information							
Doesn't eat right	27	16	17	25	32	38	50
Trouble falling asleep	32	14	26	28	39	50	60
Nightmares	26	14	17	25	25	42	55
Has aches and pains	38	8	29	40	41	54	75
Fakes being sick	27	13	21	25	33	40	45
Is afraid to go to school	18	6	8	16	25	36	30
Is picked on by other children	48	33	37	44	59	56	85
Afraid of many things	27	4	9	23	33	52	90
Very shy	26	10	17	23	35	34	65
Demands too much attention	55	40	48	54	53	72	100
Doesn't trust other people	31	10	19	28	43	52	55
Is sad or unhappy much of the time	53	17	34	54	72	68	90
Cries a lot	37	10	22	38	49	46	80
Wants things to be perfect	34	18	22	34	38	46	85
Teacher Rating and School Information							
None							
Description of Current Problem Behaviors							
Sleep disturbance:							
Has nightmares/bad dreams	29	11	23	28	37	41	50
Mother overly permissive, difficulty in setting limits	41	28	31	43	39	58	75

PSY SCALE CORRELATES	BR	30-49 n=29	50-59 n=69	60-69 n=77	70-79 n=70	80-89 n=81	90-99 n=47	100-109 n=33	≥110 n=25
Pre-Appointment Information									
Slow to first stand alone	5	0	3	1	4	9	2	12	20
Slow to first walk by self	11	3	7	8	4	15	15	15	40
Slow to speak first real words	20	10	16	12	17	24	23	30	40
Slow to toilet train	10	0	3	9	7	12	13	21	28
Refuses to go to bed	30	14	21	20	31	28	30	52	72
Trouble falling asleep	32	10	19	25	36	33	43	49	64
Has few or no friends	49	7	24	34	56	64	79	61	80
Is picked on by other children	48	28	38	34	49	57	68	55	60
Plays alone most of the time	44	7	19	15	51	59	77	67	84
Breaks things	40	17	28	38	39	35	60	46	80
Cries a lot	37	21	20	36	26	44	49	55	64
Has temper tantrums	57	41	42	57	54	64	62	67	80
Acts younger than real age	45	17	37	33	44	49	60	67	72
Says or does strange or peculiar things	42	21	21	37	39	47	64	55	84
Is often confused or in a daze	40	3	28	36	39	47	55	39	76
Daydreams a lot	41	21	23	40	41	52	47	46	68
Teacher Rating and School Information									
Repeats one idea, thought, or activity over and over	19	8	8	14	20	19	29	36	41
Has few or no friends	28	8	19	21	30	32	46	44	27
Description of Current Problem Behaviors									
Rapid mood shifts	49	39	43	46	46	40	62	66	76
Self-destructive behavior	15	3	9	16	19	14	13	21	32
Destructive of objects	38	19	24	36	33	35	61	42	72
Poor judgment/needs much supervision	53	57	42	46	46	58	55	67	84

PSY SCALE CORRELATES CONTINUED	BR	30-49 n=29	50-59 n=69	60-69 n=77	70-79 n=70	80-89 n=81	90-99 n=47	100-109 n=33	≥110 n=25
Description of Current Problem Behaviors (contd.)									
Concrete thinking beyond age expectation	22	10	14	15	20	24	31	28	53
Has few or no friends	56	21	47	49	52	66	66	84	72
Isolative (usually plays alone, stays in room, etc.)	40	4	24	29	49	45	58	71	48
Resistant to change in environment	27	29	23	21	23	26	28	35	61
Sleep disturbance: Has difficulty getting to sleep	33	7	27	27	36	28	40	58	63
Speech disturbance:									
• Phonation	8	0	7	7	4	4	11	12	33
• Echolalia	2	0	2	0	1	3	0	6	17
Overactive or agitated	28	14	21	25	24	30	38	29	61
Abnormal motor behavior (spinning, hand flapping gesturing, etc.)	4	0	3	0	4	1	4	12	28

Appendix B 165

HPR SCALE CORRELATES	BR	20-39 n=51	40-49 n=65	50-59 n=78	60-69 n=111	70-79 n=60	≥80 n=66
Pre-Appointment Information							
Clumsy or accident prone	37	20	25	27	44	47	52
Won't obey school rules	57	14	31	50	66	80	88
Picks on other children	42	8	22	30	48	67	71
Fights with other children	49	20	25	35	51	85	79
Lies	62	37	45	56	67	73	88
Steals	35	18	19	30	32	55	60
Sets fires	14	6	2	6	15	22	31
Breaks things	46	14	17	35	51	52	59
Very shy	26	53	35	28	19	23	6
Poor loser	53	31	26	53	60	67	75
Talks back to grown-ups	58	35	43	49	61	77	77
Disobeys parents	66	45	52	56	71	82	85
Can't be trusted	52	28	35	40	60	63	78
Can't sit still	61	22	34	39	77	88	89
Acts without thinking	72	37	55	65	79	90	94
Doesn't finish things (short attention span)	71	49	55	62	79	82	88
Teacher Rating and School Information							
Complains about others' unfairness and/or discrimination toward him/her	50	32	32	46	53	63	62
Doesn't conform to limits on his/her own without control from others	63	32	49	49	70	77	83
Is overactive, restless, and/or continually shifting body positions	49	19	23	39	61	60	73
Distorts the truth by making statements contrary to fact	46	19	25	36	51	61	72

HPR SCALE CORRELATES CONTINUED	BR	20-39 n=51	40-49 n=65	50-59 n=78	60-69 n=111	70-79 n=60	≥ 80 n=66
Teacher Rating and School Information (contd.)							
Disturbs other children: teasing, provoking fights, interrupting others	53	11	25	39	69	73	78
Tries to avoid calling attention to self	23	43	34	27	17	14	15
Makes distrustful or suspicious remarks about actions of others toward him/her	39	22	24	33	45	51	50
Argues and must have the last word in verbal exchanges	37	14	13	26	47	50	60
Continually seeks attention	46	22	21	30	52	63	75
Has temper tantrums	31	22	13	24	33	47	43
When teased or irritated by other children, takes out his/her frustrations(s) on another inappropriate person or thing	34	14	15	23	45	51	42
Doesn't obey until threatened with punishment	41	14	19	38	48	47	67
Openly strikes back with angry behavior to teasing of other children	42	14	21	33	43	61	65
Displays physical aggression toward objects or persons	42	14	21	30	44	71	63
Steals, things from other children	14	0	4	8	15	29	20
Doesn't engage in group activities	37	57	46	39	37	33	18
Reacts with defiance to instructions or commands	38	14	15	35	44	53	55
Doesn't pay attention in class	40	26	20	35	48	50	58
Doesn't complete homework	28	22	20	21	31	35	41
Restless/fidgety	32	14	19	19	41	45	50
Poor study skills	35	28	23	24	41	37	52

Impulsively reacts (behaves without thinking)	41	12	22	30	50	60	64
Talkative	33	4	19	22	41	48	56
Teacher rating of magnitude of problem	75	47	60	76	82	79	90
Description of Current Problem Behaviors							
Unrealistic fears	23	43	23	31	14	23	10
Destructive of objects	38	24	18	31	50	35	59
Impulsive behavior	68	31	58	59	80	76	84
Complains of poor concentration/is easily distracted	52	22	43	36	67	67	63
Often a poor sport and poor loser	43	26	25	35	44	59	68
Seeks excessive approval	42	31	29	32	47	59	51
Overly controlling/bossy	19	4	12	10	22	26	37
Described as being selfish	24	8	18	20	22	33	43
Disobedient to parents	62	36	56	53	63	78	82
Disobedient to teachers or breaks school rules	50	12	30	51	57	64	71
History of physical fights with peers	41	20	13	36	48	63	60
Complains of peer hostility and discrimination	35	24	23	25	37	52	49
Displays irresponsible behavior	47	13	39	41	60	50	63
Blames others for his/her problems	39	24	22	34	35	58	61
Teases peers	29	7	15	15	31	49	56
Lying	48	21	30	32	60	63	75
Stealing	32	21	21	18	40	47	43
Overactive or agitated	28	12	8	18	41	43	38
Compulsive or ritualistic behavior	5	18	3	4	5	3	0
Mother overly concerned or overly protective	32	52	38	44	22	32	16

SSK SCALE CORRELATES	BR	30-49 n=47	50-59 n=103	60-69 n=73	70-79 n=113	≧ 80 n=95
Pre-Appointment Information						
Is afraid to go to school	18	4	8	18	25	28
Picks on other children	42	15	32	47	45	58
Has few or no friends	49	4	15	47	68	88
Is picked on by other children	48	15	33	47	51	76
Plays alone most of the time	44	6	17	39	58	80
Fights with other children	49	17	40	46	58	68
Breaks things	15	35	42	40	56	40
Demands too much attention	55	39	42	56	59	74
Has temper tantrums	57	32	55	54	62	67
Teacher Rating and School Information						
Other children act as if he/she were taboo or tainted	25	0	22	18	29	38
Openly strikes back with angry behavior to teasing of other children	42	16	39	38	44	54
Has few or no friends	28	9	19	26	31	44
Doesn't initiate relationships with other children	34	22	25	30	41	44
Description of Current Problem Behaviors						
Overly critical of self	24	16	16	18	33	32
Expects rejection from others	49	17	38	49	52	74
Often a poor sport and poor loser	43	20	39	42	50	51
Has few or no friends	56	20	51	43	68	76
Excessive shyness	24	11	18	17	30	32

Appendix C
Criterion Frequency (%) by PIC Scale T-Score Range
II: Correlates Selected with Limited Generalizability

CHILDREN ONLY

ACH SCALE CORRELATES	BR	20-49 n=27	50-59 n=44	60-69 n=48	70-79 n=50	80-99 n=31
Teacher Rating and School Information						
Below average achievement in:						
Physical education	31	11	4	41	36	68

IS SCALE CORRELATES	BR	0-39 n=15	40-49 n=24	50-59 n=38	60-69 n=37	70-79 n=34	80-89 n=19	90-109 n=16	≥110 n=17
Teacher Rating and School Information									
Below average achievement in:									
Physical education	31	15	24	14	16	21	50	69	69
Description of Current Problem Behaviors									
Previous psychotropic medication:									
Major tranquilizers	7	0	4	0	6	3	11	19	25

SOM SCALE CORRELATES	BR	30-49 n=25	50-59 n=38	60-69 n=58	70-79 n=37	80-89 n=29	90-119 n=13

Description of Current Problem Behaviors

CORRELATES

	BR	n=23	n=33	n=47	n=42	n=32	n=22
Description of Current Problem Behaviors							
Frequent crying	37	17	19	24	49	45	77

DLQ SCALE CORRELATES

	BR	30-59 n=35	60-69 n=31	70-79 n=50	80-89 n=42	90-99 n=27	100-109 n=11	110-119 n=4
Description of Current Problem Behaviors								
Poor judgment/needs much supervision	55	13	60	56	76	60	71	75
Runs away from home	15	3	7	12	24	26	18	67

WDL SCALE CORRELATES

	BR	30-49 n=33	50-59 n=67	60-69 n=52	70-79 n=22	80-89 n=20	90-119 n=6
Description of Current Problem Behaviors							
Frequently unresponsive to surroundings	23	4	21	24	24	50	50

PSY SCALE CORRELATES

	BR	30-49 n=16	50-59 n=28	60-69 n=33	70-79 n=27	80-89 n=38	90-99 n=25	100-109 n=18	≥110 n=15
Teacher Rating and School Information									
Shuns or avoids heterosexual activities	10	7	4	0	4	9	10	39	33
Description of Current Problem Behaviors									
Sleep disturbance: Awakens early	29	13	15	26	31	24	28	39	73

MALE CHILDREN ONLY

DVL SCALE CORRELATES	BR	20-49 n=26	50-59 n=36	60-69 n=29	70-79 n=30	≥80 n=19
Teacher Rating and School Information						
Poor fine motor coordination (drawing, etc.)	21	4	14	28	27	37
Description of Current Problem Behaviors						
Retarded physical growth	7	0	6	4	11	16

SOM SCALE CORRELATES	BR	30-49 n=18	50-59 n=25	60-69 n=42	70-79 n=24	80-89 n=23	90-119 n=8
Description of Current Problem Behaviors							
Separation anxiety	10	0	4	7	13	22	25
Somatic response to stress (e.g., stomachaches)	22	6	13	22	17	48	29

WDL SCALE CORRELATES	BR	30-49 n=28	50-59 n=47	60-69 n=34	70-79 n=18	80-89 n=10	90-119 n=3
Description of Current Problem Behaviors							
Separation anxiety	10	4	4	9	22	30	33

PSY SCALE CORRELATES	BR	30-49 n=10	50-59 n=22	60-69 n=30	70-79 n=16	80-89 n=25	90-99 n=18	100-109 n=10	≥110 n=9

Description of Current Problem Behaviors

	n=11	n=6	n=21	n=16	n=23	n=24

CORRELATES

Description of Current Problem Behaviors
Chemotherapy indicated for patient:

Stimulants	44	18	13	29	40	46	88

FEMALE CHILDREN ONLY

D SCALE **CORRELATES**	**BR**	**30-49** **n=3**	**50-59** **n=9**	**60-69** **n=13**	**70-79** **n=12**	**80-89** **n=12**	**90-119** **n=11**
Description of Current Problem Behaviors							
Worries a great deal	39	0	0	46	56	44	67
Decreased appetite	14	0	0	0	9	36	27

ANX SCALE **CORRELATES**	**BR**	**30-49** **n=4**	**50-59** **n=12**	**60-69** **n=16**	**70-79** **n=12**	**80-89** **n=10**	**90-119** **n=6**
Description of Current Problem Behaviors							
Decreased appetite	14	0	0	19	9	22	23
Perfectionistic or meticulous behavior	10	0	0	0	25	10	33

ADOLESCENTS ONLY

IS SCALE CORRELATES	BR	0-39 n=31	40-49 n=63	50-59 n=42	60-69 n=36	70-79 n=24	80-89 n=18	90-109 n=12	≥110 n=5
Teacher Rating and School Information									
Has enuresis (wets the bed)	4	0	2	0	0	9	7	10	50
Utters nonsense syllables and/or babbles to self	11	4	4	9	10	14	21	36	25
Description of Current Problem Behaviors									
Nocturnal enuresis: Continuing	9	7	5	2	6	21	24	0	73

DVL SCALE CORRELATES	BR	20-49 n=50	50-59 n=72	60-69 n=60	70-79 n=37	≥80 n=12
Pre-Appointment Information						
Not fully toilet trained (wets bed, soils, etc.)	13	4	10	19	14	42

FAM SCALE CORRELATES	BR	30-49 n=36	50-59 n=59	60-69 n=72	70-79 n=47	80-99 n=17
Pre-Appointment Information						
Often skips school	41	44	25	35	54	82

Description of Current Problem Behaviors

CORRELATES

	BR	n=16	n=30	n=37	n=31	n=33	n=22	n=26	n=34
Description of Current Problem Behaviors									
Poor judgment/needs much supervision	51	30	23	53	63	46	47	57	75
Runs away from home	36	6	20	31	31	37	43	46	65
Obsessive thought pattern	8	11	30	4	11	8	0	0	0
Perfectionistic or meticulous behavior	9	31	17	14	7	0	5	4	3
History of problematic substance (drug) abuse	19	0	3	17	11	9	14	31	60

PSY SCALE CORRELATES

	BR	30-49 n=13	50-59 n=41	60-69 n=44	70-79 n=43	80-89 n=43	90-99 n=22	100-109 n=15	$\geq$110 n=10
Pre-Appointment Information									
Not fully toilet trained (wets bed, soils etc.)	13	0	15	5	9	12	18	27	50

HPR SCALE CORRELATES

	BR	20-39 n=32	40-49 n=48	50-59 n=44	60-69 n=48	70-79 n=25	80-109 n=34
Teacher Rating and School Information							
Transfer to vocational training program	4	0	0	2	6	4	15

MALE ADOLESCENTS ONLY

SOM SCALE CORRELATES	BR	30-49 n=17	50-59 n=28	60-69 n=33	70-79 n=21	80-89 n=23	90-119 n=9
Description of Current Problem Behaviors							
Headaches	27	6	15	24	43	52	11

D SCALE CORRELATES	BR	30-49 n=8	50-59 n=15	60-69 n=33	70-79 n=31	80-89 n=27	90-119 n=18
Pre-Appointment Information							
Has threatened or attempted suicide	28	0	20	21	33	33	44
Hurts self on purpose	10	0	0	3	10	19	22
Description of Current Problem Behaviors							
Expresses suicidal thoughts or ideations	25	0	15	16	28	39	39
Somatic response to stress (e.g., stomachaches)	31	13	7	25	20	48	65

... SCALE CORRELATES	n=9	n=15	n=28	n=21	n=18	n=9	n=15	n=17
Description of Current Problem Behaviors								
History of problematic substance (alcohol) abuse	13	0	4	16	6	11	20	50
Refer for outpatient individual therapy	34	67	36	52	28	33	13	6

PSY SCALE CORRELATES	BR	30-49 n=5	50-59 n=25	60-69 n=26	70-79 n=26	80-89 n=19	90-99 n=17	100-109 n=7	≥110 n=7
Description of Current Problem Behaviors									
Displays an associative (thought) disorder	3	0	0	0	0	5	0	14	29
Refer for outpatient individual therapy	34	60	48	42	27	21	35	14	14

HPR SCALE CORRELATES	BR	20-39 n=19	40-49 n=16	50-59 n=26	60-69 n=32	70-79 n=16	80-109 n=23
Description of Current Problem Behaviors							
Seems bright in many ways, but still achieves poorly in school	49	23	22	63	46	57	69
Overly conforming/passive follower	20	37	44	14	16	7	10

FEMALE ADOLESCENTS ONLY

D SCALE CORRELATES	BR	30-49 n=4	50-59 n=14	60-69 n=19	70-79 n=23	80-89 n=22	90-119 n=17
Teacher Rating and School Information							
Refers to self as dumb, stupid, or incapable	17	0	9	8	13	22	36
Expresses concern about being lonely, unhappy	32	0	9	39	19	39	57
Is hypercritical of himself	18	0	9	15	0	17	57
Description of Current Problem Behaviors							
Usually expects failure	38	0	31	21	38	40	77

FAM SCALE CORRELATES	BR	30-49 n=19	50-59 n=22	60-69 n=29	70-79 n=20	80-89 n=9
Description of Current Problem Behaviors						
Child expresses strong dislike of a member of the family	51	11	48	61	63	78
Father uses excessive physical punishment	29	20	0	40	33	100

DLQ SCALE CORRELATES	BR	30-59 n=7	60-69 n=15	70-79 n=9	80-89 n=10	90-99 n=17	100-109 n=13	110-119 n=13	≥120 n=15
Description of Current Problem Behaviors									
Seems bright in many ways, but still achieves poorly in school	38	0	27	63	0	21	73	17	64
Precocious sexual behavior or promiscuity	21	0	8	0	0	6	22	56	67

ANX SCALE CORRELATES	BR	30-49 n=13	50-59 n=20	60-69 n=30	70-79 n=24	80-89 n=9	90-119 n=3
Teacher Rating and School Information							
Refers to self as dumb, stupid, or incapable	17	0	7	15	24	22	67
Expresses concern about being lonely, unhappy	32	0	29	25	43	44	67
Is hypercritical of himself	18	0	7	10	24	33	100

FEMALES ONLY

ACH SCALE CORRELATES	BR	20-49 n=25	50-59 n=49	60-69 n=40	70-79 n=28	80-99 n=17
Teacher Rating and School Information						
Child has repeated a grade	13	0	6	15	29	18

IS SCALE CORRELATES	BR	0-39 n=17	40-49 n=37	50-59 n=43	60-69 n=16	70-79 n=19	80-89 n=11	90-109 n=8	$\geq$110 n=8
Description of Current Problem Behaviors									
Frequent fights with siblings	29	0	27	20	29	21	56	63	67

PSY SCALE CORRELATES	BR	30-49 n=14	50-59 n=22	60-69 n=21	70-79 n=28	80-89 n=37	90-99 n=12	100-109 n=16	$\geq$110 n=9
Pre-Appointment Information									
Slow to first sit up	10	7	0	0	7	8	17	13	67
Slow to first crawl	13	0	9	5	11	11	17	19	67
Teacher Rating and School Information									
Becomes hysterical, upset or angry when things do not go her way	36	20	19	15	22	55	64	50	50

INDEX

Achenbach, T.M. — 14, 23
Achievement Scale (ACH) — 10, 23, 24, 26, 27, 29, 36-37, 51, 54-55, 70-71, 75, 90, 101, 102, 104, 112, 150-151, 172, 182
Adjustment Scale (ADJ) — 10, 16, 23, 26, 29, 34-36, 52-53, 69-70, 88, 90, 101, 104, 148-149
Age, effects of — 12, 23-26
Alexander, R.S. — 16, 29
Anxiety Scale (ANX) — 12, 23, 24, 26, 29, 43-44, 49, 61, 80, 96, 101, 102, 112, 113, 162, 175, 181

Base rate, correlate — 10, 19, 100, 146-182
Bishop, C.H. — 10
Boerger, A.R. — 16
Butkus, M. — 1

Case studies — 102-113
Clinical lore — xvii
Code type — 1, 113
Computer applications — xiv, xv, xvii
Configural patterns — xiv
Construct validity — 14, 26
Correlate frequency — xiv, 14-21, 145-182
Correlates, age-specific — 14, 27, 33, 34, 35, 36, 37, 38, 40, 41, 42, 44, 45, 47, 48, 52, 53, 54, 56, 57, 60, 61, 62, 63, 65, 68, 69, 70, 71, 72, 74, 75, 77, 78, 80, 81, 83, 84, 172-173, 176-177
clinician — 26-27, 67-85
parent — 26-27, 31-49
primary — 19, 21
secondary — 21
selection — 13-21
sex-specific — 14, 27, 32, 33, 34, 35, 36, 38, 39, 41, 42, 43, 45, 47, 48, 52, 53, 54, 56, 57, 59, 60, 61, 62, 65, 68, 69, 72, 76, 78, 80, 81, 83, 84, 182
sex/age specific — 14, 27, 40, 58, 59, 61, 74, 75, 76, 77, 78, 79, 80, 81, 82, 83, 174-175, 178-181

teacher — 26-27, 51-65
total sample — 13-14, 26-27, 32, 33, 34, 35, 36, 37, 38, 39, 40, 41, 42, 43, 44, 45, 46, 47, 48, 52, 54, 55, 56, 57, 59, 61, 62, 63, 65, 68, 69, 70, 71, 72, 73, 74, 75, 76, 77, 78, 79, 80, 81, 82, 83, 84, 146-168
unique — 16
Criterion data, clinician — 3-5, 136-143
parent — 2-3, 120-127
teacher — 2-3, 128-135
Cutting scores — xiv, 16

Dahlstrom, W.G. — 13
Darlington, R.B. — 10
Defensiveness Scale (DEF) — 10, 16, 23, 24, 26, 27, 29, 34, 88, 89, 101, 111, 147
DeHorn, A. — 1
Delinquency Scale (DLQ) — 12, 14, 16, 19, 21, 23, 24, 26, 29, 41-42, 48, 49, 59-61, 77-79, 84, 88, 94-95, 100, 101, 102, 107, 112, 113, 159-160, 173, 177, 179, 181
Depression Scale (D) — 11, 23, 24, 26, 29, 39-40, 49, 59, 75-76, 93, 101, 102, 112, 113, 157, 173, 175, 178, 180
Development Scale (DVL) — 11, 16, 23, 24, 26, 27, 29, 38, 57-58, 73-75, 91-92, 101, 102, 112, 154-155, 174, 176
Developmental milestones — 1, 2-3, 31, 35, 36, 37, 38, 43, 45-46, 48, 92, 98, 102, 105, 107, 109, 110, 123, 148, 150, 152, 154, 163, 182
Diagnoses, Group for the Advancement of Psychiatry — 7-9, 10, 87

F Scale (F) — 10, 23, 26, 29, 33-34, 52, 68-69, 89, 101, 147
Family Relations Scale (FAM) — 11-12, 16, 23, 26, 29, 41, 76-77, 94, 101, 102, 104, 107, 112, 113, 158, 176, 180

Gdowski, C.L. — xiv, xv, 1, 23, 29
Generalizability, limitations to — xiv, 10, 13, 21, 87, 113
Graham, J.R. — 16
Gynther, M.D. — 13, 26

Haloperidol — 113
Hathaway, S.R. — xiii, xvii
Hryhorczuk, L. — 1
Hyperactivity Scale (HPR) — 12, 23, 24, 26, 29, 46-48, 49, 51, 62-64, 82-84, 98-99, 101, 102, 104, 107, 111, 113, 165-167, 175, 177, 179

Informant, PIC — xiii, 12
Intellectual Screening Scale (IS) — 11, 23, 24, 26, 27, 29, 37, 55-57, 72-73, 75, 91, 101, 102, 112, 113, 152-153, 172, 176, 182
Interpretive guidelines — 29, 87-101

Klinedinst, J.K. — xiii, xv, xvii, 1

L Scale (L) — 10, 16, 23, 24, 26, 29, 32, 34, 52, 68, 88, 89, 101, 111, 146
Lachar, D. — xiii, xiv, xv, xvii, 1, 13, 16, 29
Lapouse, R. — 14, 23
Lilly, R.S. — 16
Lithium carbonate — 113

Meehl, P.E. — 19
Methylphenidate — 104, 110, 113
MMPI — xiii, xiv, xvii, 26
Monk, M.A. — 14, 23

Personality Inventory for Children (PIC) — 10-12
Primary enformant — 1, 31
Profile interpretation — 101-102

Psychosis Scale (PSY) — 12, 23, 26, 29, 45-46, 62, 81-82, 88, 97-98, 101, 102, 111, 112, 113, 163-164, 173, 174, 177, 179, 182

Quay, H.C. — 14, 23
Quay, L.C. — 14, 23

Race — 5, 6
effects of — 12-13, 23-26
Referral source — 5, 9, 101
Response sets, deviant — xiii, 12, 89, 101
Rosen, A. — 19

Scale methodology, empirical — 10-13, 29
rational — 10-13, 29
Seat, P.D. — xiii, xv, xvii, 1
Sechrest, L. — 19
Sex, effects of — 12-13, 23-26, 53
Sex/age groups — 13-15, 21, 29
Social Skills Scale (SSK) — 12, 23, 24, 26, 29, 43, 48-49, 65, 84-85, 99, 101, 102, 112, 113, 168
Socioeconomic status — xiii, 5, 10
Somatic Concern Scale (SOM) — 11, 23, 24, 26, 29, 39, 75, 93, 101, 102, 112, 113, 156, 172, 174, 178
Study subjects — 5-10

Test-taking attitude, see response sets
Thioridazine — 107, 113

Walker Problem Behavior Checklist — 3
Werry, J.S. — 23
Wirt, R.D. — xiii, xv, xvii, 1, 12, 23
WISC — xv
Withdrawal Scale (WDL) — 12, 23, 24, 26, 29, 43, 49, 61, 79-80, 96, 101, 102, 112, 113, 161, 173, 174
WPPSI — xv